Link to the '30s

Kay Connors and Karen Earlywine

Link to the '30s

MAKING THE QUILTS WE DIDN'T INHERIT

Martingale®
& COMPANY

Link to the '30s: Making the Quilts We Didn't Inherit
© 2009 by Kay Connors and Karen Earlywine

That Patchwork Place® is an imprint of
Martingale & Company®.

Martingale & Company
20205 144th Ave. NE
Woodinville, WA 98072-8478 USA
www.martingale-pub.com

Printed in China
13 12 11 10 09 08   8 7 6 5 4 3 2 1

Library of Congress Cataloging-in-Publication Data
is available upon request.

ISBN: 978-1-56477-879-6

CREDITS

President & CEO • Tom Wierzbicki

Editorial Director • Mary V. Green

Managing Editor • Tina Cook

Developmental Editor • Karen Costello Soltys

Technical Editor • Nancy Mahoney

Copy Editor • Marcy Heffernan

Design Director • Stan Green

Production Manager • Regina Girard

Illustrator • Laurel Strand

Cover & Text Designer • Shelly Garrison

Photographer • Brent Kane

MISSION STATEMENT

Dedicated to providing quality products
and service to inspire creativity.

DEDICATION

This book would not have been possible without our Idaho friend, Lola Bennett, who has a talent for finding treasures in odd places and sharing them with us. She generously gave us a box of old clippings and patterns from which seven of the quilts featured here were created, and she subsequently served as our head cheerleader.

ACKNOWLEDGMENTS

Thanks to our indulgent spouses and children, who support our quilting efforts, to the designers of all those wonderful 1930s reproduction fabrics, and to the bright and supportive editorial staff at Martingale & Company.

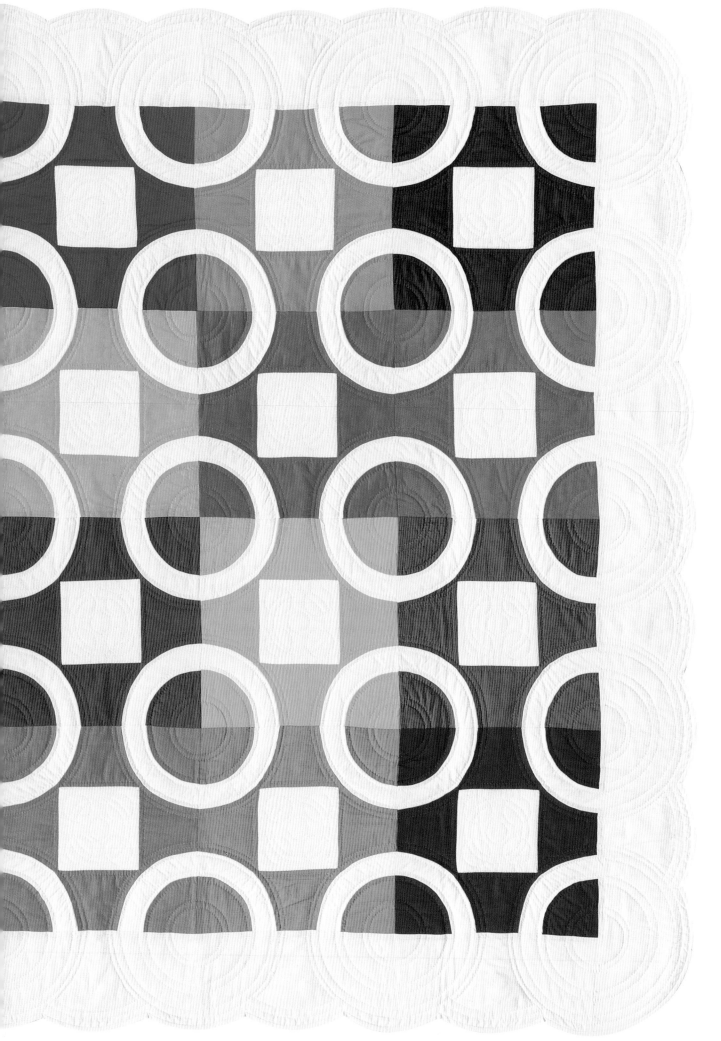

Contents

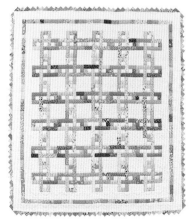

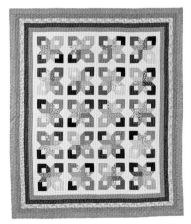

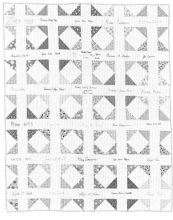

 # Introduction

Summers for us when we were children were spent bouncing between our two grandmothers in Texas. One was stiff and staid, and the other had a home full of eclectic things: flowers planted in an old cowboy boot, a matchstick holder fashioned from a wasp's nest sitting invitingly on the coffee table, a bobble-head donkey that "ate" the green coconut "grass" off of birthday cakes, and, most importantly, quilts. Each June when we arrived, she had a new crop of magical things, the most exciting of which were the quilts. She sold insurance door-to-door and met lots of folks each week, forming relationships that got her foot in the door when they needed to dispose of family treasures, and thus her house was stuffed with mustache cups, Depression glass, and quilts.

How could we not love these beautiful old creations made from feed sacks and leftover calicos used for aprons and kitchen curtains? Good women with high hopes made these wonderful bed coverings, many times ordering the patterns from their local newspapers. But more often than not they clipped the ads from the paper, putting them away until they had the few pennies needed to send for them, and those are the ones that you'll find in this book.

One grandmother showed us the colorful excitement of quilts, and, luckily, the other one taught us to sew. With adolescence came sewing clothes for ourselves, and later we sewed for our daughters, and being true gals of our generation, we saved the remnants for our quilts. When the time came to start quilting, we found very few resources available. We had to learn everything on our own, from drafting a block to burying a knot. Now books and packaged patterns are everywhere, but we still return to those old quilts from our childhood memories and bless the fabric designers who have given us a wide variety of reproduction 1930s fabrics.

Whenever we come across an old quilt or an ad with a pattern that's new to us, we experience that familiar excitement and can't wait to make it. And now we want to introduce you to some of our old favorites as well as some new finds. Since we love the old 1930s quilts, we try to make them the way we know the women of the time made them, with lots of muslin background, a wild display of colored prints and bright solids, and loads of hand quilting.

By the way, in her retirement that wonderful grandmother with the quilts opened an antique shop, and one by one the treasures of our childhood memories found new homes with people who we hope loved them as much as we did.

That "other" grandmother left a surprise for us. We found a wonderful Lone Star quilt top among her possessions and finished it for her, and it now belongs to Kay, but it stays in our jointly owned quilt cottage in the hill country of Texas, so Karen can enjoy it as well. You can see it, too, as the backdrop of our author portraits in this book.

Now we are making the quilts that we didn't inherit and loving the challenge!

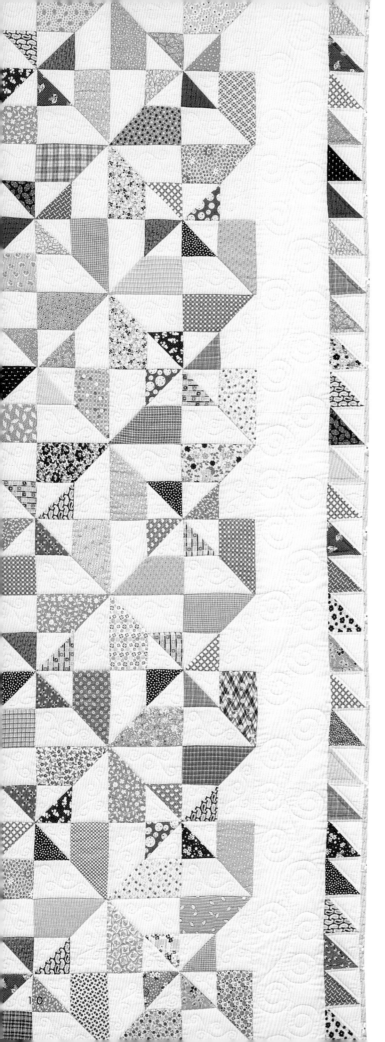

 # Making Do

A few years ago, we fell hopelessly in love with 1930s reproduction fabrics and started to amass a large collection. We made a few quilts with them from time to time, but our fabric stashes kept growing while we yearned for projects worthy of cutting into them. One old pattern was discovered at a garage sale, others fell into our laps, and in antique shops we found there were tired old quilts that cried out to be re-created.

We live far apart, in southwestern New Mexico and the Idaho panhandle, but we spend part of every year together, shopping for endless additions to our stashes and talking Depression-era quilts. As our children left the nest, we had more time and talked more often of writing this book. Separately we found ourselves decorating with quilts to complement antiques and collectibles. Our visits to each other made us realize that we were on a parallel path in our quilting pursuits.

Already competitive quilters (and competitive with each other—we *are* siblings!) and achievement oriented, it was not a far reach to decide to write a book using the found patterns and our passion for the times and techniques of the 1930s.

The Great Depression is best described by this old axiom: Use it up, wear it out, make it do, or do without.

Times were hard during the thirties and early forties, and people had to adhere to this old adage. They looked around to see how they could relieve their situation without spending money they didn't have. Yet they needed to continue the heritage of needlecraft that was always part of the fabric of women's lives. Quilting is one of the most tangible examples we have of this humble yet artistic process.

Use it up. Most women of the time had at least rudimentary sewing skills for clothing construction, mending, and household decoration. This industry, in most cases, resulted in fabric remnants piling up. Feed and flour sacks were even more plentiful and not to be wasted.

Wear it out. Many clothing articles wore out unevenly, leaving areas of relatively good fabric for other items. Often aprons were made from old less-worn sections of dresses, and men's shirts offered scraps that could be recycled.

Make it do. Money was scarce and dreams that required money couldn't be realized. Women clipped quilt-block patterns from newspapers that offered, for a few cents, the entire pattern and instructions. The day those pennies were expendable may have never come, but the newspaper ad was not thrown away, the dream never given up on, and often the quilter had to make the quilt from just that much of the plan.

Or do without. This was not an option for the dedicated quilter, whether hoping to provide simple warmth for a family member's bed or create a masterpiece. Quilting provided an artistic outlet for women often overwhelmed by their circumstances. They combined use it up, wear it out, and make it do to keep from doing without.

This is not to say that new fabrics and patterns weren't purchased, that women didn't share patterns and knowledge, that incredible quilts did not come out of this era, but times were hard, and most women had to be resourceful in order to quilt. (Women from that era were known to hold in disdain quilters in later times who could and would purchase and cut up perfectly good fabric to make a quilt!) Often the quilt top was completed, but there it ended. Fabric for backing, and batting to fill the quilt were not always attainable. Completed quilts often have sacking on the back with surviving printing informing us of the products that the bags once contained. We see many of these quilts, or we see a beautiful quilt top that has only been tied or finished without batting. We have seen examples of quilts that are so thin that air seems to have been the only stuffing. Others are thick and lumpy, and close examination shows that raw cotton was used with seeds and particles of husks still present. One quilt had an old wool military blanket inside, and sometimes the batting in a quilt is simply another older, more worn quilt put back into service as batting.

Whether fabric was purchased or simply left over, there was a wide array of wonderful pastel prints and a rainbow of solids to match. Fabric selection for scrap quilts

was not problematic in the thirties; you could hardly go wrong with any combination of these prints and solids. Juxtaposed against bleached or unbleached muslin, these prints fairly sang. Not all quilts from this period were made from scraps; some were limited to a few fabrics selected to achieve a particular effect, almost always set on muslin for an economical background.

You will find a variety of challenges in this book, but you can also find several quilts for the less-experienced quilter. Techniques range from simple construction and appliqué, to curved seams, to complex blocks with multiple set-in pieces. The confident beginner will enjoy the quilts that use more rotary cutting and straight-line piecing as in "Reunion Memories" (page 88) and "Double Windmill" (page 32), while the advanced quilter will welcome the challenge of multiple techniques and intricate patterns in "Star Flower" (page 38), "Stroll around the Garden" (page 56), and "Sweet Insanity" (page 80). For the intermediate quilter we offer "Rings 'n' Things" (page 64), "Jeweled Wedding Ring" (page 24), "Stars in the Attic" (page 72), and "Chain Link" (page 48). In all cases, the result will be worth the effort.

Because we found only the block drawings for most of these quilts, we had to imagine what the settings, borders, and edges should look like. We added detail on the borders and edges that you may choose to omit, but it will require yardage adjustments, which we have not provided. Leave the border of "Rings 'n' Things" plain, without scallops; trade the prairie points of "Chain Link" for a simple binding; omit the Dresden border from "Stroll around the Garden" or the "snow-cone" border that finishes "Star Flower."

We are so glad these quilters of the 1930s persevered; doing whatever it took to create their wonderful quilts, shaping our memories and our continuing love of the quilts they made and dreamed of making. Today we often complain that our lives are hectic, but we challenged ourselves, and now we challenge you to step back and invest time and patience into efforts that will reward you with heirloom quilts that would have made the women of seventy-plus years ago proud. And don't you really want to make the quilts you didn't inherit?

Quiltmaking Basics

In the 1930s, quilters were lucky to have rudimentary tools that were necessary for garment making: needle and thread, thimble, scissors, ruler, pencil, and often a sewing machine. Fabric came from feed or flour sacks, remnants of clothing, and/or purchased yard goods. When we started to quilt in the 1970s, it was impossible to buy 100%-cotton fabric of the quality required to duplicate the old quilts, books were scarce, and tools had not been developed as we know them today. Aren't we the lucky ones to now have ample supplies of good fabric and tools the quilters of the 1930s—or the 1970s for that matter—could never have imagined?

FABRIC

Fabric is the most important consideration in your quilt. Start with only high-quality 100%-cotton material. Mixing fabrics of different content may result in areas of your quilt that reflect light oddly, stretch or sag differently, and worsening with age. High thread count, colorfastness, true printing, and straight grains are all the qualities you need in your material. Fabric purchased from quilt shops, while perhaps more expensive, is more reliable, and you don't want to put a lot of effort into your quilt and regret the small economies.

Our quilts utilize lots of print scraps; when you have them, use them. Otherwise purchase fat eighths or fat quarters in a wide array of 1930s prints and colors for eight of our quilts (one quilt uses only solids). In our estimation, you can never overbuy for your stash!

To prewash or not to prewash—isn't that the big question? Karen prewashes her fabric, smooths, and folds it for storage on her shelves, pressing if necessary. Kay does not prewash, can't bear to lose that new fabric look, and likes the finish and stability of new fabric. She does, however, test stronger colors by rubbing a soft white cloth on the surface of the fabric to look for color transfer. Most '30s fabrics are pastel and can be used with or without prewashing. However, if you don't prewash, be sure to use a dye-grabber in the washer the first time you launder the quilt. If some excess dye bleeds and causes staining, wash again with a bleach-for-colors product.

Shrinkage is an issue. Better fabrics are not likely to shrink a significant amount, but this cannot be said for bargain fabric or looser weaves. We have taken shrinkage into consideration in our yardage requirements and recommend that you prewash all fabrics to be on the safe side.

Muslin is a major component of our quilts and the most authentic fabric for the backgrounds, many of the block pieces, and the backing for all of our quilts. Buy good-quality muslin, both in 45" width and the widths that are recommended for your quilt backing. Because of the transparency of muslin, be vigilant in trimming raveled threads and dog-ears (little corners of seams that stick out). You may also need to trim seam allowances so that the darker fabric colors don't show through the lighter fabrics. Although we love muslin, you may prefer to use a cream solid in place of muslin for the quilt top or the backing.

SUPPLIES

We hold the old quilters in high esteem, but we will use any tools or modern techniques that facilitate the process. The methodology of the 1930s is important in the quest to replicate the look and feel of the original quilts, but we are not gluttons for punishment.

Sewing machine: Know your machine and how it relates to quilting. Ensure that you have a sharp needle, the right size for woven cottons. Dulled, burred, or slightly bent needles can damage your fabric or distort your seams. Consider loading several bobbins before beginning a project to avoid interruption. You will, in all cases, use a ¼" seam allowance. If unsure about the precision of your seam allowance width, practice on junk fabric or notebook paper and make adjustments.

Cutting tools: Both scissors and a rotary cutter can be used. Some of the pieces in our quilts require cutting with scissors. Make sure that your scissors are sharp and short bladed. Cutting multiple layers in this instance is not recommended. Utility scissors are used for cutting out templates. Thread nippers are great for clipping sewing threads at the sewing machine and stray threads throughout the process.

Rotary cutters are the quilter's version of pizza cutters, very sharp, and available in a variety of sizes and ergonomic styles. Larger-diameter blades are used for straight lines and for cutting multiple layers, and the smaller ones are best for cutting soft curves and one or two layers of fabric. Use a rotary-cutting mat and acrylic rulers that you are most comfortable with. We like a 6" x 24" ruler for cutting strips and a 6" x 12" ruler for crosscutting squares and rectangles. Squaring up your blocks will require a 12" or larger square ruler. A 6" square ruler is useful for trimming partial blocks and making clean-up cuts as shown on page 14. Several yardsticks are essential for squaring up large quilts.

Needles and thread: We hand quilt and hand appliqué using very small needles known as Betweens. The smaller and finer the needle, the smaller the stitch. We prefer a size 12 or 13, but if you are new to hand quilting, you may find them too small, and a size 10 may better suit you. Use a 100%-cotton thread for piecing and appliqué and a good-quality hand-quilting thread, which is prewaxed to be a bit stiffer and less likely to tangle or fray. Thread conditioners are also readily available. For the quilts in this book, off-white or very pastel thread should be used because of the muslin backgrounds.

Pins: We recommend decorative flat-head pins because you can place your ruler atop them for rotary cutting, and they are hard to lose. A few pieces in this book have two straight sides and one curved edge, and pinning to hold them is important before making the straight cuts. Safety pins have multiple uses in quilting: pin basting your quilt together, securing pieces that will be worked with for a longer period, and marking areas that you may want to return to for further attention.

Seam ripper: This invaluable tool will help you safely remove stitches to make minor adjustments from incorrectly sewn seams.

Template material: When rotary cutting is not feasible, templates for appliqué and piecing can be made from many different materials including template plastic, lightweight cardboard, or heavy cardstock. It does not matter what kind of material you make your template from as

long as it is a sturdy material that can withstand numerous uses. To avoid cutting your template through repeated use, draw around the template onto the fabric before cutting, rather than cutting around the template itself.

Marking tools: There are many products available for marking your quilts, but be cautious and informed. Water-soluble pens, chalk, pouncing powder, and pencils are all good choices. Avoid anything with permanent ink or an oil base. Test your choice of marking tool on a scrap piece of fabric so you will know how the mark will be removed before using it. The finer the line you can use, the less you will have to remove.

Thimbles: One or more thimbles are essential for hand quilt construction. A lightweight thimble is best for hand piecing and appliqué. One or more reinforced thimbles are needed for handquilting. Some hand quilters push with the middle finger when quilting in one direction and switch to a thimble on their thumb to quilt in a different direction.

Miscellaneous tools and supplies: Several other tools will come in handy:

- A lint roller picks up all those loose threads from around the sewing machine or the quilt frame as well as from your clothes. A last-minute cleanup of the back of your quilt top is made easier with a lint roller.

- Tweezers, hemostats, or a tiny crochet hook will remove threads protruding through seams.

- Bag balm or ointment for sore fingers.

- Freezer paper should always be on hand for appliqué and temporary stabilizing.

- Quilter's thumbtacks may be used to secure the edges of the backing to the quilt frame.

- A small appliqué iron (also called a Mini Iron) by Clover is best for pressing appliqué edges. It heats up quickly and is easy to use on the smallest details.

- A digital camera can capture block or quilt layouts for future reference and can also be used to gain distance perspective.

- Surplus yardage is useful to make extender strips for quilt tops or to test your cutting and piecing skills.

ROTARY CUTTING

1. Making sure that your fabric is smooth and without wrinkles, fold the fabric in half, matching the selvages. Lay the fabric on a mat with the fold nearest you; be sure there are no twists along the fold and the fabric is smooth underneath. Align a square ruler with the fold of the fabric and place your longest straight ruler to the left of the square so that the raw edges of the fabric are covered. (Reverse this procedure if you are left-handed.)

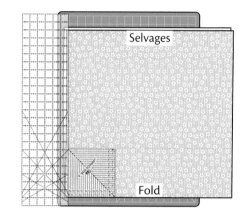

2. Set the square ruler aside, and then cut along the right edge of the long ruler. Be sure to roll the rotary cutter away from you. Remove the long ruler and gently remove the waste strip.

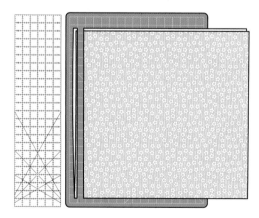

3. Now you are ready to start cutting strips from your fabric. Align the desired strip width with the cut edge of the fabric and carefully cut a strip. For example, to cut 2"-wide strips, place the 2" mark on the edge of the fabric. Continue cutting strips until you have the required number of strips. Periodically stop and square up your fabric edge again before continuing.

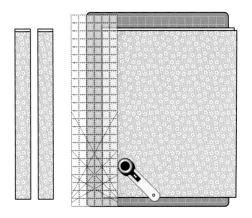

4. To cut squares and rectangles, cut strips in the required widths. Using a small ruler (typically 6" x 6" or 6" x 12") and placing the ruler on the left as before, trim the selvage ends of the strips. You are ready to cut pieces as required.

MACHINE PIECING

A ¼" seam allowance is standard in all of our patterns. We can't stress enough the importance of maintaining an accurate ¼" seam allowance. The Leaning Tower of Pisa doesn't appear to lean at the base, but it sure manifests itself at the top of the tower, and this can happen in your quilts if your seam allowance is consistently too narrow or too wide. That tiny fraction of an inch adds up, resulting in blocks that won't fit together.

Although straight seams are predominant, several special piecing techniques must be used to achieve the desired effect in our more challenging projects.

Set-In Pieces and Y Seams

Several quilts in this book require set-in pieces and/or Y seams, which share the same technique. The key is transferring the dots from the patterns onto the template material and marking the dots (or matching points) on the fabric piece. To sew a fabric piece into the opening created when two angled pieces are joined, making a three-way intersection, follow these three steps:

1. Place the two angled pieces right sides together, aligning the raw edges and matching the dots. Sew the seam, starting at the outside edge and stopping at the dot with a small backstitch.

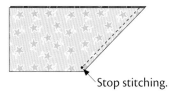

Stop stitching.

2. Pin one edge of the angled unit to one edge of the piece to be set in, right sides together. Use a straight pin to match up the dots and pin the two pieces together. Starting with a small backstitch at the dot, sew to the outside edge of the piece as indicated by the arrow.

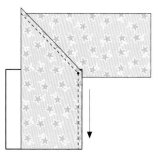

3. Align the edge of the second angled unit with the adjacent edge of the set-in piece, align the dots, and pin as before. Starting with a small backstitch at the dot, sew to the outside edge of the piece as indicated by the arrow. Press the seam allowances as indicated.

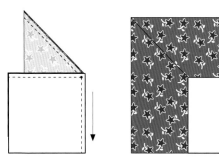

Curved Seams

Don't be intimidated by curves or arcs! Four of the quilts in this book feature them, from the little arcs that create the flower petals in "Star Flower" (page 38) or the posies in "Stroll around the Garden" (page 56) to the larger circles of "Rings 'n' Things" (page 64) and the gentle arcs of "Jeweled Wedding Ring" (page 24).

Four components make up a well-sewn, uniform curve: accurate cutting, correctly oriented grain line, clear marking by any means, and exact pinning.

Pay careful attention to the grain-line markings on the pattern pieces. When a grain line is indicated on the template, be sure to align the arrow with either the lengthwise grain or the crosswise grain of the fabric; do not align the arrow with the bias grain. For more details on making plastic templates, refer to "Templates" on page 17.

Mark center points and any other points that may help you achieve an accurate seam. We like to fold the piece in half along the curved edge and finger-press to mark the midpoint; then fold again to mark the quarter points. You can also mark with pencil or chalk on the wrong side of the fabric. Some template patterns include positioning dots, be sure to transfer the dots from the patterns onto the template material. Once you've cut out the templates, use a 1/8" hole punch to make a small hole to mark each dot. Use a sharp pencil in the center of each hole to transfer the dots to the wrong side of the fabric.

Placing the piece with the inside arc on top, push a positioning pin through a matching point on the wrong side of the top piece. Insert the pin through the corresponding point on the bottom piece. If there is more than one matching point, insert a pin through each point. (This will help you to avoid tucks by keeping your top fabric from pushing ahead of your stitches.) Pin each important point and any more that will ensure a good seam. You may choose to clip slightly into the seam allowance on curves. For one of our quilts, "Star Flower," we've included clip-

ping points on the template patterns. We find that a greater number of small clips are preferable to deep clips that are too close to the seam line.

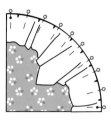

Make sure to maintain a consistent 1/4" seam allowance and stretch or ease both fabrics, as needed, as you sew the seam. With the needle down, be sure to lift the presser foot regularly to allow the fabric to flatten out. The tighter the curve, the more important this becomes. Press the completed unit and check for tucks along the seam line.

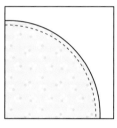

Hand Piecing

You may choose to hand piece the tight curves of "Stroll around the Garden" or "Star Flower." If you are more comfortable with this technique or enjoy a take-along project, hand piecing is simple and may give you a better result. Simply substitute a very short running stitch for the line of machine stitches, making sure to have a knot at each end of your row of stitches.

Chain Piecing

When sewing many identical pieces, it is advantageous to feed pairs of pieces under the presser foot of your sewing machine without cutting the thread or lifting the presser foot. Once the first seam has been made, immediately feed another pair of pieces through the machine and repeat with the rest of the pairs. A few stitches will separate your units.

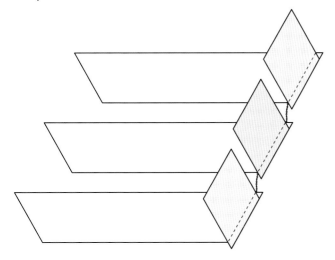

You can turn your chain of pieces and add another piece to each unit, maintaining your chain. This is a tremendous time-saver and keeps your work organized. When all of the pieces are sewn, remove the chain from the machine and clip the threads between the pairs of sewn pieces.

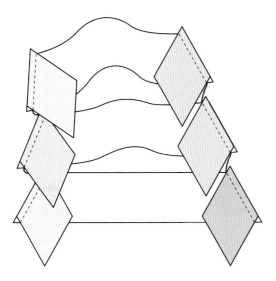

Pressing

When pressing straight seams, press the seam flat from the wrong side to embed the stitches. Flip the top fabric open and press again from the right side, pressing the seam allowance in the direction indicated in the illustrations and making sure not to stretch or distort the seam. Press curved seams in the direction indicated in the illustrations. Press after sewing each piece to your block.

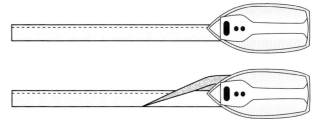

TEMPLATES

You'll need to make templates for some of the pieces that cannot be rotary cut. Template patterns are given with the projects that require them. Piecing template patterns include the seam allowance, which is shown as part of the template. Seam allowances are not included on templates for appliqué pieces.

To make a template, place a piece of template plastic (or other template material) over the required pattern. Use a fine-tip permanent marker to trace the line of the shape exactly onto the plastic. If the pattern has a fabric grain line, mark the line on the template. Use utility scissors to cut out the template *exactly* on the drawn lines. Mark the right side of the template. You need to make only one plastic template for each pattern piece. Always place the right side of the template *facing up* on the right side of the fabric, unless instructed otherwise.

Some projects require a reverse image of the template. If you need a reverse image, simply flip the template over so that the right side of the template is *facing down* on the right side of the fabric.

BASIC APPLIQUÉ

The appliqué needed to make the quilts in this book is a simple one-layer appliqué—one piece of fabric stitched over the top of another to form the design. You don't need to fear curves or points when appliqués are properly prepared and stitched. There are many different appliqué methods; try the method we prefer or use your favorite appliqué technique. We use a freezer-paper technique that yields a smoother, more accurate line or curve.

Make a plastic template of each appliqué shape. Place the template *right side facing up* on the paper (non-shiny) side of a piece of freezer paper; use a sharp pencil to trace the shape onto the freezer paper. Cut out the freezer-paper template on the drawn lines. Freezer-paper templates should always be cut exactly on the line because the seam allowance will be added when the shapes are cut from fabric. You'll need several freezer-paper templates of each shape. Each freezer-paper template can be used several times.

Place the plastic template *right side facing down* on the wrong side of the chosen fabric. Draw a line around the template with a sharp pencil, leaving about ½" between each shape for seam allowance. Cut out each shape, adding a scant ¼" for seam allowance around the entire shape. Clip the seam allowance on all curves as needed, stopping two or three threads from the line to leave an intact fabric edge for pressing the seam allowance onto the shiny side of the freezer-paper template.

On the wrong side of each fabric shape, position a freezer-paper template in the center of each shape, with the shiny side of the paper facing up. Use pins to hold the template in place as needed. Using an appliqué iron, carefully press the seam allowance over the edge of the freezer-paper template onto the shiny side of the template. Always press the seam allowance toward the center of the shape to avoid puckers or pleats along the edge of your appliqué. Move slowly around the shape, easing around the curves to achieve a smooth edge. *This method differs from those where you press the shiny side*

of the paper to the wrong side of your fabric; we use the freezer paper to hold the appliqué edges down until they are stitched.

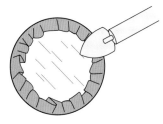

We have provided guides for easy placement of the appliqué pieces. Marking the placement of the appliqué shapes on the background fabric will allow you to repeat your design uniformly from block to block. After marking, position the prepared appliqué shapes on the background fabric and pin in place.

Appliqué Stitch

There is only one stitch to know in hand appliqué, and it is quite simple. Use a single strand of thread approximately 18" long that closely matches the fabric color of the appliqué. Tie a knot in one end. Hide the knot in the fold made by the seam allowance, bringing the needle out along the folded edge.

Make the first stitch into the background fabric, directly below where the needle emerged. Run the needle not more than ⅛" under your background fabric, parallel to the edge of the appliqué. Bring the needle up through the background fabric, catching one or two threads of the folded edge of the appliqué. Very gently tug the thread with each stitch. On the front all you should see are very small dots of thread outlining the appliqué.

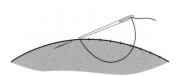

When the appliqué is complete, carefully make a slit in the background fabric behind each appliqué to expose the freezer-paper template. Use tweezers or the point of a long pin to gently remove the template.

Appliqué tends to draw up the background fabric, so we recommend using the slit as an entry point to carefully cut away the background fabric behind the appliqué shape, leaving approximately ¼" seam allowance.

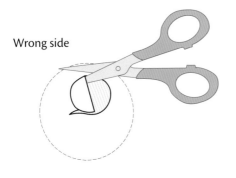

Wrong side

Squaring Up Blocks

Once you've completed your quilt blocks, it's time to square them up. If your blocks vary slightly in size, trim the larger blocks to match the size of the smallest block. To square up a block, line up the vertical and horizontal seam lines of the block with the center lines of the desired-size square on the square ruler. For example, the centerline for an 11½" square is the 5¾" line. Cut the first two sides of the block. Turn the block around and cut the other two sides. Make sure you have a full ¼" seam allowance beyond the outside points and any other important design elements. If needed, remove any dog-ears and excess threads. Press the block.

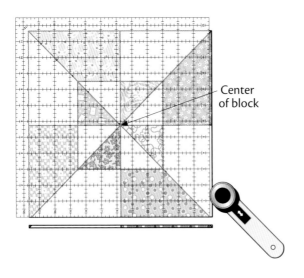

Center of block

QUILT TOP ASSEMBLY

All the quilts in this book are set in straight rows. Arrange the blocks in rows as shown in the assembly diagram for your project. In general, the blocks will be sewn together in rows, with the seam allowances pressed in opposite directions from row to row. Then the rows are sewn together. Press the seam allowances all in one direction, unless instructed otherwise.

Borders

Border construction is specific to each quilt in this book. Several of our quilts have pieced- or folded-edge treatments. Instructions for these borders are included in the project instructions.

For quilts with straight-cut corners (sometimes referred to as butted borders), the measurements for the border strips are given in the cutting instructions for each project. The border strips are a few inches longer than you'll actually need, so you can trim them to the correct length once you know the dimensions of your quilt top. To find the correct measurement for the border strips, always measure the quilt top through the center. This helps keep your quilt square.

1. Measure the width of your quilt top through the center. Mark the center of the border strips and the center of the top and bottom of the quilt top. Trim two border strips to this measurement. Pin the borders to the quilt top, matching centers and ends, easing if necessary. Sew the borders in place with a ¼"-wide seam allowance. Press the seam allowance toward the border strip, unless instructed otherwise.

2. Measure the length of the quilt top through the center including the just-added borders. Trim two border strips to this measurement. Mark, pin, sew in place, and press the border strips in the same manner as before. Repeat this method for each additional border.

FINISHING

Press the entire quilt, checking the wrong side for seam allowances that may have flipped over in your final construction. Remove any loose threads or other debris and make one final inspection for dark threads or seam allowances that must be trimmed to ensure that they do not show through to the front. Make any adjustments necessary.

Marking the Quilting Lines

We strongly recommend that all marking be done at this point. Quilting designs are provided for some projects. You can use them to make stencils, or use a light box to mark your quilt top. Of course, you can also use a favorite stencil.

Using your quilting design and the marking tool of choice, draw all of the lines that you plan to quilt. If grid quilting is being marked, start in the middle of one side, marking and checking often to ensure that the angle and spacing is consistent. Use a long ruler and the 45°-angle line on the ruler to mark square grids and diagonal lines for quilting.

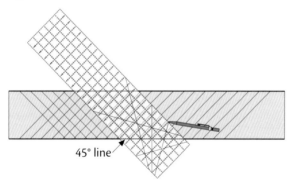

45° line

Layering the Quilt

Now you are ready to sandwich your layers together. You'll need your finished quilt top, batting, and backing. The batting and backing should be a minimum of 3" larger on all sides than the quilt top. We have given yardage measurements for muslin 90" or wider for backing, which is available in most quilt shops and will save you a great deal of time. Backing fabrics in '30s reproduction prints are also available.

Our quilts feature low-loft batting with mixed cotton and synthetic fibers. If you are an experienced quilter, use the batting you enjoy working with. Before basting your quilt, unfold the batting and allow it to relax for about 24 hours, or place it in your dryer on a cool setting for a few minutes to eliminate wrinkles or bunching.

Basting

1. Spread the backing wrong side up on a clean, flat surface. Anchor it with masking tape or, if placing it on a carpet, secure it with T-pins. Do not distort the fabric by overstretching, but smooth out all wrinkles and once again remove any loose threads or other debris.

2. Spread the batting over the backing, smoothing out any wrinkles.

3. Center the prepared quilt top over the batting, again smoothing out any wrinkles and making sure the quilt-top edges are parallel to the edges of the backing.

4. For hand quilting, baste with needle and thread, starting in the center and working diagonally to each corner. Continue basting in a grid of horizontal and vertical lines 6" to 8" apart. To finish, baste around the edges about ⅛" from the quilt-top edge.

For machine quilting, baste the layers with #2 rustproof safety pins. Place pins 4" to 6" apart, trying to avoid areas where you intend to quilt. Finish by machine basting around the edges about ⅛" from the quilt-top edge.

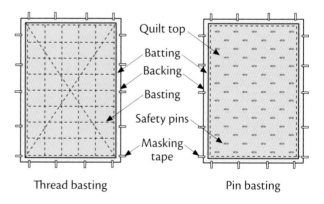

Quilt top
Batting
Backing
Basting
Safety pins
Masking tape

Thread basting   Pin basting

Hand Quilting

For hand quilting, you need strong short needles (called Betweens), hand-quilting thread, and a thimble to fit the middle finger of your sewing hand. You may also want to use a thimble or protection for your hand underneath the quilt. We both have floor frames for our larger quilts, but use hoops for smaller projects. The frame allows for even stretching, producing a flat, square quilt. The use of a hoop requires care not to stretch or pleat the backing, and you must start in the middle of the quilt.

Thread a needle with a single strand of quilting thread 18" to 24" long. Make a knot in the end and insert the needle through the top layer and into the batting about 1" from the place where you want to start stitching. Pull the needle out at the point where the quilting will begin. Gently tug until the knot makes a distinctive pop through the quilt top and into the batting, place your other hand underneath the quilt to determine that the knot did not slip through to the back. Make the first stitch straight down through all three layers; with the underneath hand feel the needle point with the tip of your finger as a stitch is taken. While the needle is still in the layers, use your thimble to rock the needle up through all layers. Continue this rocking motion between your middle finger and thumb until you have three or four stitches on your needle (called loading the needle), and then pull the needle through and make the thread taut. Insert the needle again straight down and repeat to achieve consistency in length and appearance. We all admire tiny stitches, but consistency is the foremost aim of good hand quilting. Practice makes perfect! To end a line of quilting, make a small knot as close to the quilt top as possible, tuck the needle through the quilt top and into the batting, and bring your needle back to the surface. Gently tug on the thread until the knot pops into the batting. Holding the needle with slight tension on the thread, snip the thread close to the quilt surface. The end of the thread will slip back into the quilt layers.

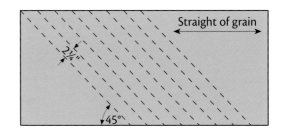

Hand-quilting stitch

We are admirers of machine quilting and recognize the beauty and time-saving result, but this book is about heirloom quilts made the "old-fashioned" way. We hope that you can hand quilt your creation, but the choice is truly yours.

Binding

You are ready for the last step, binding your quilt. Binding finishes the edges of the quilt and seals the quilt sandwich, but not all quilts have binding. Our "Chain Link" quilt on page 48 uses prairie points to finish the edges, and instructions for that technique are included with the project.

Binding cut on the straight grain works for all quilts with straight edges. We cut 2¼"-wide strips and use a double-folded binding, called French binding, for all of our quilts. When binding a quilt that has rounded corners or scalloped borders, you must use bias-cut binding.

1. Cut the binding strips as instructed for each quilt. Straight binding is cut crosswise, but bias binding is cut at a 45° angle as shown.

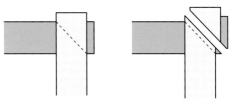

2. Sew the binding strips together to make one long strip. Join strips at right angles right sides together, and stitch across the corner as shown using a ¼" seam allowance. Press the seam allowances open.

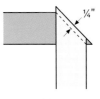

Joining straight-cut strips

Joining bias strips

3. Cut one end of the long binding strip at a 45° angle as shown. Press the strip in half lengthwise, wrong sides together and raw edges aligned.

Fold line
Right side
Wrong side

4. Trim the batting and backing even with the quilt top. Use your longest ruler and a square ruler to make the quilt square and straight.

5. Using a ¼" seam allowance, starting on the bottom edge of the quilt at least 15" from a corner, and leaving a 6" tail, stitch the binding to the quilt, being careful not to stretch either the binding or the quilt. Keep the raw edges even with the quilt-top edge. Stop stitching ¼" from the corner and backstitch.

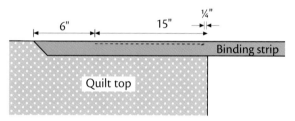

6" 15" ¼"
Binding strip
Quilt top

6. Remove the quilt from the sewing machine. Fold the binding straight up, away from the quilt so the fold forms a 45° angle. Fold binding back down onto itself, even with the edge of the quilt top to create an angled pleat at the corner. Begin stitching ¼" from

the corner, backstitching to secure the stitches. Repeat the process on the remaining edges and corners of the quilt.

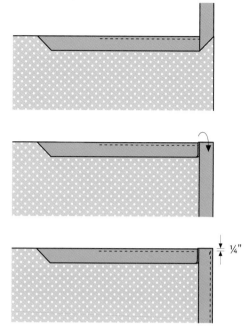

¼"

7. Stop stitching approximately 12" from the starting end of the binding strip and backstitch. Remove the quilt from the machine. Place the quilt on a flat surface and layer the beginning (angled) tail on top of the ending tail. Mark the ending tail where it meets the beginning tail. Make a second mark ½" to the right of the first mark.

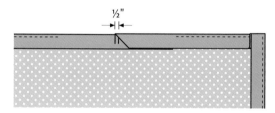

½"

8. Open the ending tail strip and align the 45° line of a small Bias Square® with the top edge of the open binding strip. Place the corner of the ruler on the

second mark. Cut the ending tail strip along the edge of the ruler as shown. The ends of both binding strips will form 45° angles and overlap ½".

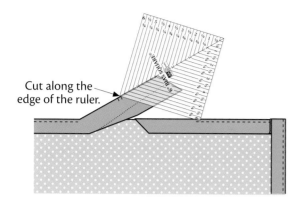

Cut along the edge of the ruler.

9. Place the binding ends right sides together, aligning the angled raw edges and matching the crease lines as shown. Fold the quilt out of the way and stitch the ends together using a ¼" seam allowance. Press the seam allowance open, refold the binding, and then press the fold. Finish stitching the binding to the quilt top.

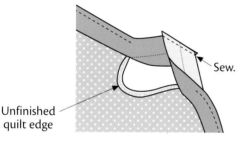

Sew.

Unfinished quilt edge

10. Turn the binding to the back of the quilt. Using matching thread and making sure the machine stitching line is covered, hand stitch the folded edge to the backing. Fold the binding to form a miter at each corner.

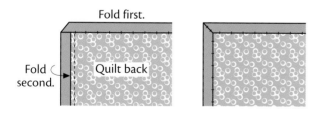

Fold first.

Fold second.

Quilt back

Bias Binding

When binding a quilt that has curved edges we recommend some special treatment. When the quilting is finished, baste around the edges ¼" from the edge of the quilt top. This will stabilize the edge. Then trim the batting and backing ¼" beyond the line of stitching, even with the quilt top. Apply the binding as described above; of course you won't have corners to miter, but the other steps for attaching and finishing the binding are the same, with the following exception for inside corners on scalloped edges. As you approach the inside corner, clip almost to the stitching line. This allows you to stretch the inside corner apart at the clipped point and makes binding easier.

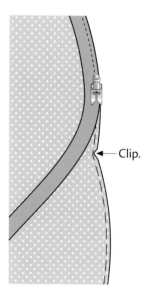

Clip.

Once the binding is stitched to the quilt, turn the binding to the back of the quilt, stretching the inside corners apart, and pin the binding in place. When you let go of the corner, a natural tuck will appear. Hand stitch the binding in place, sewing a stitch or two in the tuck to hold it tightly in place.

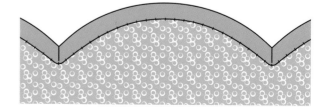

McCall had a line of packaged patterns in the 1930s, and this is one of the finest examples we have ever seen. People comment that "the form is so familiar, but the pattern certainly isn't." We all know the old Double Wedding Ring pattern, constructed with segments in the arcs and without appliqué, which appears to be daunting. We made this one in "that pink" from the era and embellished it with "gems" created from reproduction fabrics.

We had the original pattern which included tissue paper iron-on transfers, but no directions. The rings and centers of the blocks are very large pieces coupled with simple, one-layer appliqués that use up lots of tiny scraps. This is a fun project that results in an eye-popping quilt.

Jeweled Wedding Ring

Finished Quilt: 87½" x 107¼"

MATERIALS

Yardage is based on 42"-wide fabric.

8½ yards of unbleached muslin for melon units and background

8 yards of pink solid for arcs, small circles, and binding

3⅝ yards *total* of assorted 1930s reproduction prints for appliqués

3½ yards of 108"-wide unbleached muslin for backing*

94" x 114" piece of batting

Freezer paper

Template plastic

*If using 42"-wide unbleached muslin, you'll need 8⅝ yards (3 widths pieced horizontally).

CUTTING

All measurements include a ¼"-wide seam allowance. Template patterns for pieces A, B, C, and D appear on pages 28–30. For detailed instructions, refer to "Templates" on page 17.

From the unbleached muslin, cut:
20 pieces with template A
49 pieces with template C
98 pieces with template D

From the pink solid, cut:
325" of 2¼"-wide bias strips
98 pieces with template B

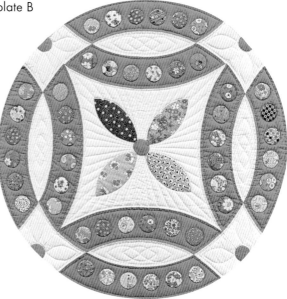

Pieced, appliquéd, and quilted by Kay Connors and Karen Earlywine.

APPLIQUÉING THE PIECES

We recommend that you appliqué pieces E and F to all of the A and B pieces before sewing the pieces together to make the quilt top. This makes it easier to mark the appliqué placement, and the appliqué is less cumbersome than trying to work on the completed quilt top. Plus it makes this an easy take-along appliqué project.

1. Refer to "Basic Appliqué" on page 18 as needed. Prepare the E and F pieces for appliqué using the patterns and following the instructions on page 31.

2. To mark the A pieces for appliqué placement, use a long ruler and a removable marker to draw diagonal lines from corner to corner in both directions, so that the lines cross in the center of each A piece.

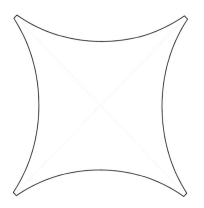

3. Position a pink E piece in the center of each A piece and appliqué in place. Position F pieces so that one end is touching the pink circle and the other end is aligned with a marked diagonal line as shown. Appliqué four F pieces around the center of each A piece.

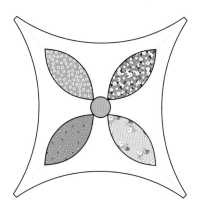

4. Using the plastic template B piece (with the circles cut away) and a removable marker, mark the placement for the E pieces on a pink B piece. Appliqué six assorted E pieces to each B piece.

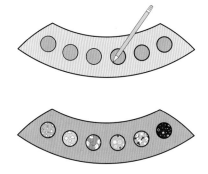

ASSEMBLING THE QUILT TOP

When the appliqué is completed, you'll sew the pieces together to make the quilt top. Refer to "Curved Seams" on page 16 as needed.

1. Fold each appliquéd B piece and muslin C piece in half and finger-press to mark the midpoints. Pin and sew a B piece to one side of each C piece to make a partial melon unit. Press the seam allowances toward the C piece. Make 49.

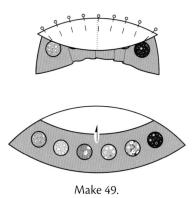

Make 49.

2. Sew a D piece to each end of the remaining B pieces. Press the seam allowances toward the B piece. Make 49.

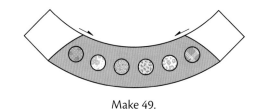

Make 49.

3. Sew one unit from step 2 to each partial melon unit as shown to make a full melon unit. Press the seam allowances toward the C piece. Make 49 melon units.

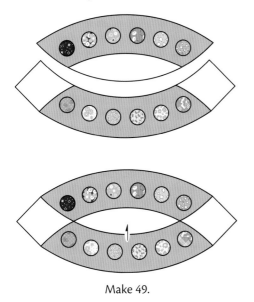

Make 49.

4. Fold each melon unit and appliquéd A piece in half and finger-press to mark the midpoints. Pin a melon unit to one side of an A piece right sides together, matching the midpoints. With the melon unit on top, sew the pieces together. Press the seam allowance toward the melon unit.

5. Repeat step 4, sewing a melon unit to the three remaining sides of the A piece. Make one. This is the only unit composed of four melon units and one A piece.

6. Repeat step 4 to make 7 units using three melon units and one A piece.

7. In the same manner, make 12 units using two melon units and one A piece.

8. Arrange the units as shown in the quilt assembly diagram. Sew the units together. Press the seam allowances toward the melon units.

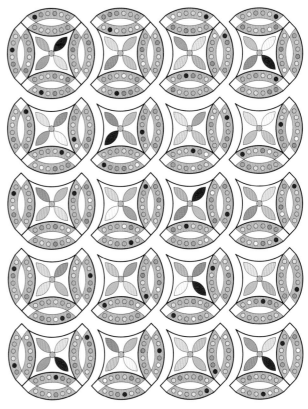

Quilt assembly

COMPLETING THE APPLIQUÉ

1. Referring to the photo on page 25 for placement, appliqué pink E pieces over each seam intersection where four D pieces meet in the quilt-top center.

2. Along each side of the quilt top, appliqué pink E pieces over each intersection where three D pieces meet. Stitch around three-quarters of the circle; trim the excess fabric even with the melon units.

3. At each corner of the quilt top, appliqué pink E pieces over each intersection where two D pieces meet. Stitch around half of the circle; trim the excess fabric even with the melon units.

QUILTING AND FINISHING

Refer to "Finishing" on page 20 for details as needed.

1. Mark the quilting lines using the quilting design suggested or your own favorite quilting design.

2. Layer the quilt top with batting and backing; baste.

3. Hand quilt following the marked lines. Quilt ¼" from the seams and closely around each appliqué piece.

4. Use the pink 2¼"-wide bias strips for binding.

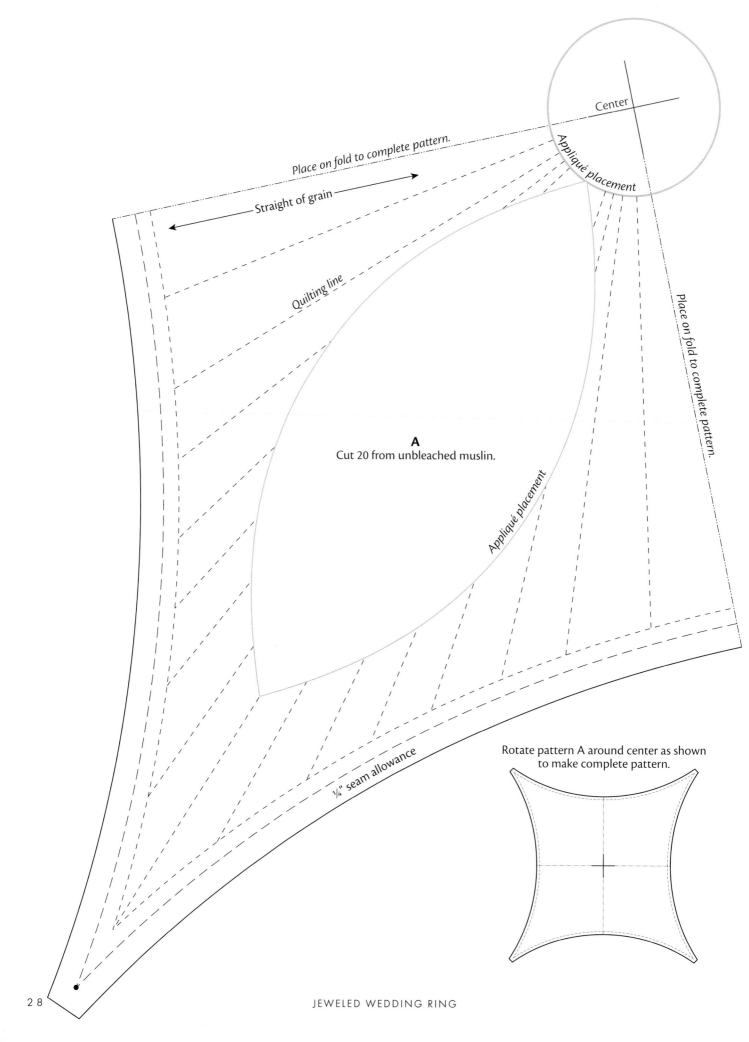

Center

Appliqué placement

Place on fold to complete pattern.

Straight of grain

Place on fold to complete pattern.

Quilting line

A
Cut 20 from unbleached muslin.

Appliqué placement

¼" seam allowance

Rotate pattern A around center as shown
to make complete pattern.

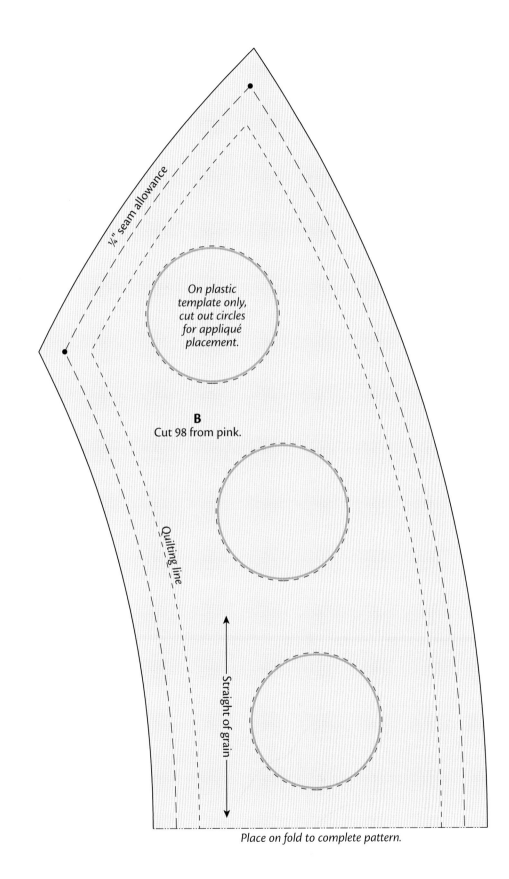

¼" seam allowance

On plastic
template only,
cut out circles
for appliqué
placement.

B
Cut 98 from pink.

Quilting line

Straight of grain

Place on fold to complete pattern.

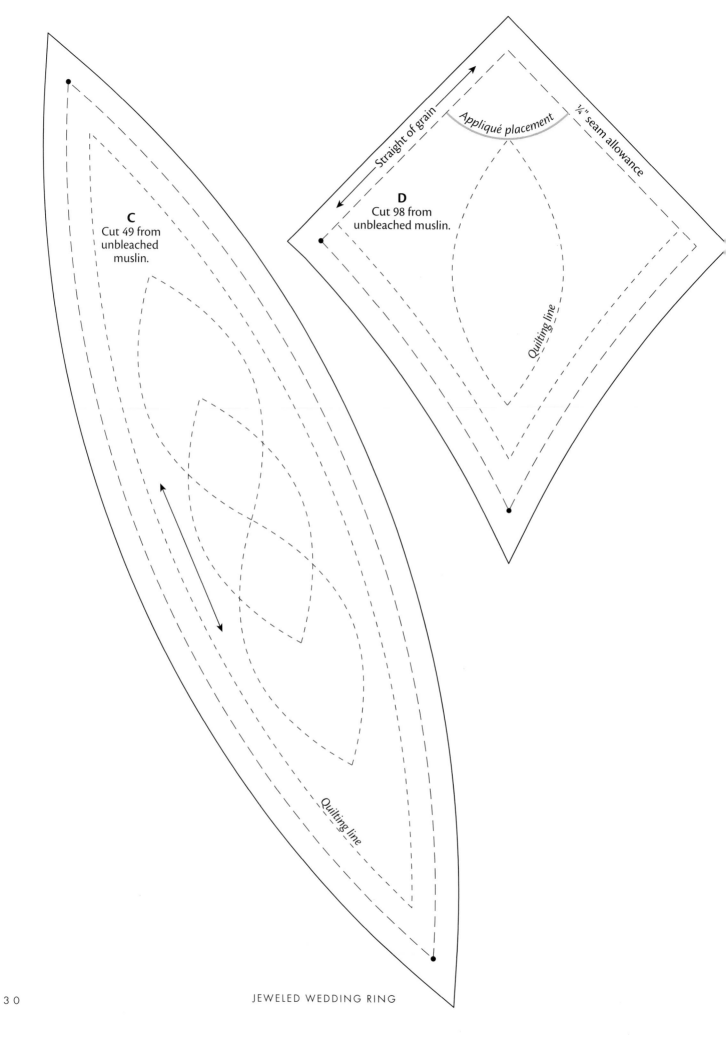

C
Cut 49 from
unbleached
muslin.

Quilting line

Straight of grain

Appliqué placement

¼" seam allowance

D
Cut 98 from
unbleached muslin.

Quilting line

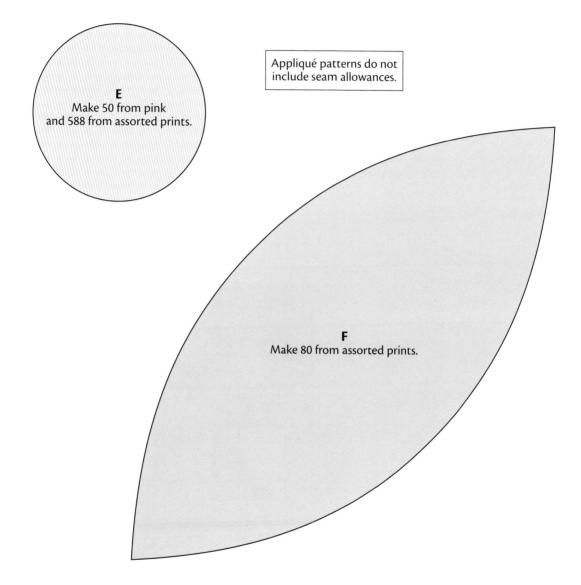

E
Make 50 from pink
and 588 from assorted prints.

Appliqué patterns do not
include seam allowances.

F
Make 80 from assorted prints.

When published in the *Spokane Daily Chronicle* newspaper, Alice Brooks's Depression-era "Double Windmill" pattern was described as "simple." It is an easy quilt with only two pattern pieces, but it has the potential to be a showcase for a large collection of prints, feeding the eye of an appreciative viewer. In the dust-bowl years of the Depression, the windmills were especially important to pump much-needed water and offered a companionable sound to remote farmhouses. Hand-quilted swirls of wind bring Karen's windmills to life.

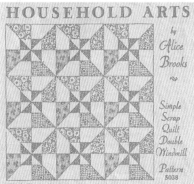

Double Windmill

Finished Quilt: 83" x 94" • Block Size: 11" x 11"

MATERIALS

Yardage is based on 42"-wide fabric.

6½ yards of unbleached muslin for blocks and borders

4 yards *total* of assorted 1930s reproduction prints for blocks and outer border

¾ yard of yellow print for binding

3 yards of 90"-wide unbleached muslin for backing*

89" x 100" piece of batting

Template plastic

If using 42"-wide unbleached muslin, you'll need 8¼ yards (3 widths pieced horizontally).

Pieced and quilted by Karen Earlywine.

DOUBLE WINDMILL

CUTTING

All measurements include a ¼"-wide seam allowance. Template pattern for piece A appears on page 36. For detailed instructions, refer to "Templates" on page 17.

From the assorted 1930s reproduction prints, cut a total of:

146 squares, 3⅝" x 3⅝"; cut once diagonally to yield 292 half-square triangles

168 pieces with template A

From the *lengthwise grain* of the unbleached muslin, cut:

2 strips, 6" x 92"

2 strips, 6" x 70"

From the remaining unbleached muslin, cut:

21 strips, 3¼" x 42"; cut into 168 pieces with template A*

146 squares, 3⅝" x 3⅝"; cut once diagonally to yield 292 half-square triangles

From the yellow print, cut:

10 strips, 2¼" x 42"

*NOTE: If you're using muslin or a solid fabric, you don't need to cut reverse pieces; however, if you substitute a fabric that has a right and wrong side, cut 168 pieces with template A reversed.

MAKING THE BLOCKS

1. Sew each muslin half-square triangle to a print A piece as shown. Press the seam allowances toward the A piece. Sew each print half-square triangle to a muslin A piece. Press the seam allowances toward the print triangle. Refer to "Chain Piecing" on page 16 to make the sewing process quicker, if desired. Make 168 of each unit.

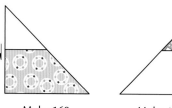

Make 168.   Make 168.

2. In a pleasing mix of colors, arrange eight units as shown. Pin and sew two units together along the long edges, matching the seams, to make a square unit. Be careful not to stretch the bias edges as you stitch. Press the seam allowances toward the print A piece. Make four square units for each block (168 total).

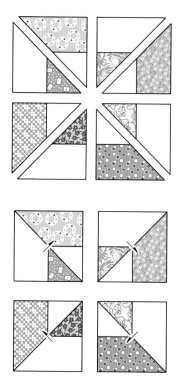

3. Using a ruler, trim each square unit to measure 6" x 6" by placing the 45° line on your ruler along the diagonal seam. Be sure to trim off the dog-ears.

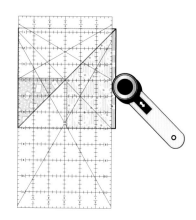

4. Sew the square units together in pairs to make a half block. Sew two half blocks together, matching the seams, to complete the block. Make a total of

42 blocks. Trim them to 11½" x 11½", referring to "Squaring Up Blocks" on page 19 as needed.

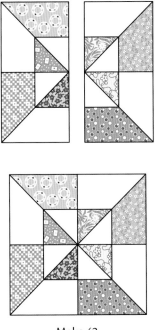

Make 42.

ASSEMBLING THE QUILT TOP

1. Arrange the blocks in seven rows of six blocks each as shown in the quilt assembly diagram. Rearrange the blocks until you are pleased with the color placement.

2. Sew the blocks into rows. Press the seam allowances in alternate directions from row to row. Stitch the rows together. Press the seam allowances in one direction.

3. Refer to "Borders" on page 19. Using the muslin 6"-wide strips, measure, cut, and sew the shorter strips to the top and bottom of the quilt top, and then the longer strips to the sides of the quilt top. Press all seam allowances toward the newly added borders. The quilt top should measure 77½" x 88½" for the outer border to fit properly.

4. Sew the remaining print half-square triangles and muslin half-square triangles together along their long edges to make 124 half-square-triangle units. Press the seam allowances toward the print triangles.

5. Sew 30 half-square-triangle units together for the top border. Be sure all of the print triangles are facing in the direction shown in the assembly diagram. Repeat to make the bottom border.

6. Sew 32 half-square-triangle units together in the same manner for each side border. Make two side-border strips.

7. Referring to the quilt assembly diagram, pin and sew a side-border strip to the right and left sides of the quilt top. Press the seam allowances toward the muslin strips.

8. Sew the border strips from step 5 to the top and bottom of the quilt top. Press the seam allowances toward the muslin strips.

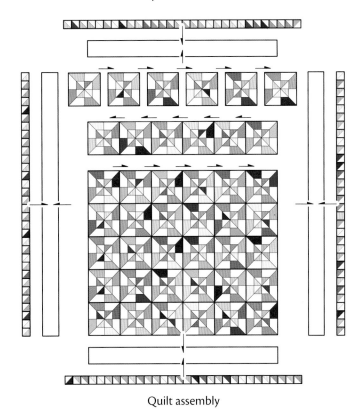

Quilt assembly

QUILTING AND FINISHING

Refer to "Finishing" on page 20 for details as needed.

1. Mark the quilting lines using the quilting design suggested or your own favorite quilting design.

2. Layer the quilt top with batting and backing; baste.

3. Hand quilt following the marked lines and stitch in the ditch around all of the print pieces.

4. Use the yellow 2¼"-wide strips for binding.

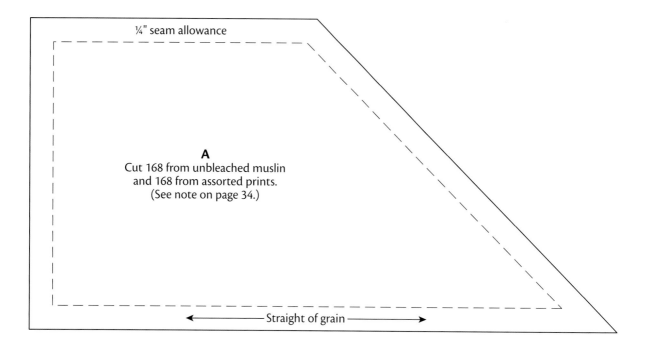

¼" seam allowance

A
Cut 168 from unbleached muslin
and 168 from assorted prints.
(See note on page 34.)

←———— Straight of grain ————→

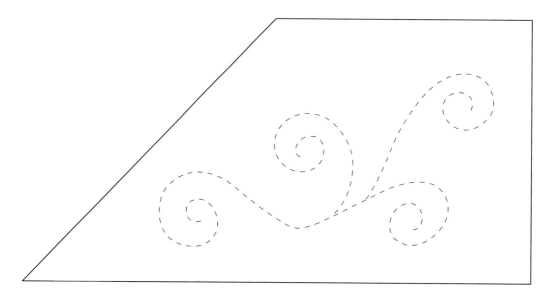

Quilting design for muslin A reversed units

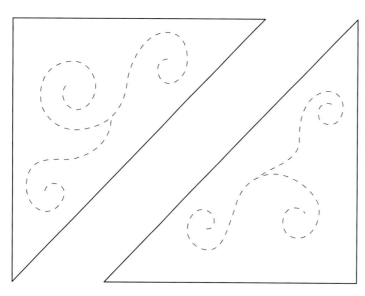

**Quilting designs for muslin
half-square triangles
in Windmill blocks**

Quilting design for border
Enlarge 125%.

Alice Brooks's line of quilt patterns was a fixture in newspapers in the 1930s, and this is one of her most attractive offerings. Not a pattern for the faint of heart, it offers a challenge for any quilter who wants to make a true heirloom quilt complete with "snow-cone" borders and lots of quilting.

This is a great quilt to showcase a couple of strong print fabrics and utilize a large scrap collection for the diamonds. Kay made this one several years ago and was rewarded with a big ribbon at the annual quilt show in Sisters, Oregon. It will be a winner for you, too!

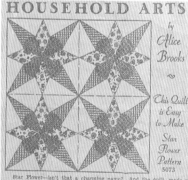

Star Flower

Finished Quilt: 82½" x 101½" • Block Size: 9½" x 9½"

MATERIALS

Yardage is based on 42"-wide fabric.

6½ yards of unbleached muslin for blocks and outer border

4 yards of green print for blocks, outer border, and binding

3¾ yards of yellow print for blocks, inner border, and corners of outer border

2¼ yards *total* of assorted 1930s reproduction prints for blocks

3⅜ yards of 90"-wide muslin for backing*

89" x 108" batting

Template plastic

*If using 42"-wide unbleached muslin, you'll need 8¼ yards (3 widths pieced horizontally).

Pieced and quilted by Kay Connors.

STAR FLOWER

CUTTING

All measurements include a ¼"-wide seam allowance. Template patterns for pieces A, B, C, D, E, F, and G appear on pages 44–46. For detailed instructions, refer to "Templates" on page 17.

When cutting the pieces it's important to pay attention to the grain lines marked on all of the templates. Although there are bias seams in the block, the outside of each block will be on the straight of grain to prevent the block from stretching.

From the unbleached muslin, cut:

7 strips, 6½" x 42"; cut into 94 pieces with template F

51 strips, 3" x 42"; cut into 504 pieces with template C*

From the *lengthwise grain* of the yellow print, cut:

2 strips, 3" x 93"

2 strips, 3" x 74"

252 pieces with template A

4 pieces with template G

From the green print, cut:

475" of 2¼"-wide bias strips

252 pieces with template B

98 pieces with template E

From the assorted 1930s reproduction prints, cut a total of:

252 pieces with template D

*NOTE: If you're using muslin or a solid fabric, you don't need to cut reverse pieces; however, if you substitute a fabric that has a right and wrong side, cut 252 pieces with template C and 252 pieces with template C reversed.

MAKING THE BLOCKS

1. Refer to "Curved Seams" on page 16. With right sides together, pin one yellow A piece to a green B piece. Align the raw edges and match the dots, clip-

ping the curves as indicated. Sew the seam and press the seam allowances toward the A piece. Make 252.

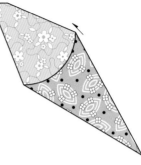

Make 252.

2. Aligning the raw edges and matching the dots, sew two muslin C pieces (one regular and one reversed, if applicable) to adjacent sides of each A/B unit as shown, starting at the outside edge and stopping at the dot with a small backstitch. Make sure the straight of grain on the muslin C piece is always along the outside edge of the block. Press the seam allowances toward muslin pieces. Make 252.

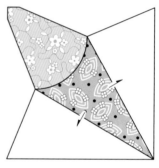

Make 252.

3. Refer to "Set-In Pieces and Y Seams" on page 15. With right sides together, sew one print D piece to the left side of each unit from step 2. Align the raw edges and match the side dots. Press toward the D piece. Make 252 units.

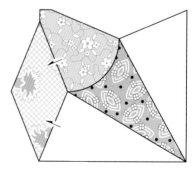

Make 252.

4. Arrange two units from step 3 as shown. Place the units right sides together with raw edges aligned, matching the C and D dots. Sew the first seam, starting at the outside edge and stopping at the dot with a small backstitch. Keeping the units right sides together and matching the A and D dots, sew seam 2, starting and stopping with a small backstitch. Then, starting with a small backstitch, sew seam 3 to complete the half-block unit. Repeat to make a second half-block unit. Press the center seam allowances in the half-block units in opposite directions so they will interlock and reduce bulk when the block is finished.

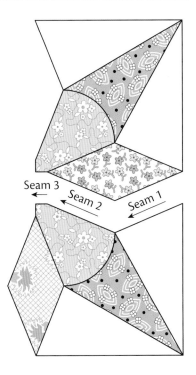

5. Place the two half-block units right sides together, align the raw edges, and match the dots. Starting at the outside edge, sew seam 1, stopping with a small backstitch. Sew seam 2, starting and stopping with a small backstitch. Sew seam 3 and seam 4, starting and stopping each seam with a small backstitch. Then

starting at the outside edge, sew seam 5, stopping with a small backstitch. Press the seam allowances open. Press the entire block flat.

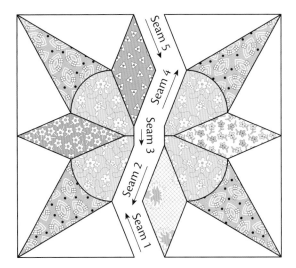

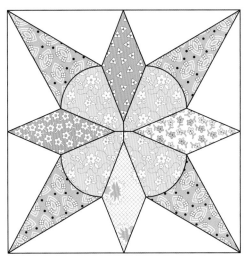

Make 63.

6. Repeat steps 4 and 5 to make a total of 63 blocks. Trim each block to 10" x 10", referring to "Squaring Up Blocks" on page 19 as needed.

ASSEMBLING THE QUILT TOP

1. Arrange the blocks in nine rows of seven blocks each as shown in the quilt assembly diagram.

2. Sew the blocks into rows. Press the seam allowances in alternate directions from row to row. Sew the rows together. Press the seam allowances in one direction.

3. Refer to "Borders" on page 19. Using the yellow 3"-wide strips, measure, cut, and sew the shorter strips to the top and bottom of the quilt top, and then the longer strips to the sides of the quilt top. Press all seam allowances toward the newly added borders. The quilt top should measure 72" x 91" for the outer border to fit properly.

MAKING THE PIECED BORDER

1. Aligning the raw edges and matching the dots, sew the green E pieces and the muslin F pieces together as shown. Make sure there is a ¼" seam allowance beyond the points of the muslin pieces and the green pieces as shown. Sew 22 green E pieces and 21 muslin F pieces together to make a border strip. Make two border strips. Press the seam allowances toward the green pieces.

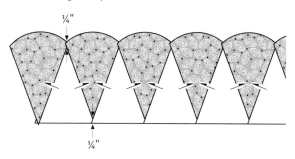

2. Sew 27 green E pieces and 26 muslin F pieces together to make a border strip. Make two side-border strips. Press the seam allowances toward the green pieces. Aligning the raw edges and matching the dots, sew a yellow G piece to both ends of each side border strip as shown. Press the seam allowances toward the green pieces.

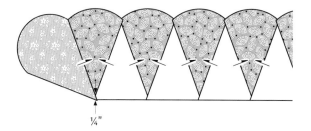

3. On the wrong side of the yellow border, mark a dot on each corner ¼" from the raw edge, for placement of the pieced border. Fold each border strip in quarters, lightly crease the folds on the muslin side of the border, and mark the creases with pins. Then fold each side of the quilt top in quarters, lightly crease the folds, and mark with pins.

4. On one short end of the quilt top, with right sides together and raw edges aligned, pin a border strip from step 1 to the quilt top, matching the corner dots on the yellow border with the dots on the green pieces and matching the pins along the raw edges. Sew the seam, starting and stopping at the dots with a small backstitch and easing or stretching slightly as needed. Press the seam allowances toward the yellow border. Repeat to sew a border strip to the opposite short end.

5. With right sides together and raw edges aligned, pin and sew the side-border strips to the quilt top in the same manner as before.

6. At each corner, aligning the raw edges and matching the dots, pin the green E piece to the yellow G piece. Start at the dot with a small backstitch and sew to the outside edge; press.

Sew seam.

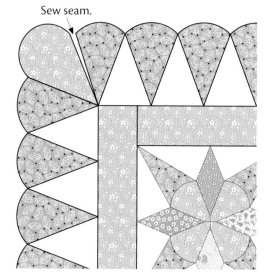

QUILTING AND FINISHING

Refer to "Finishing" on page 20 for details as needed.

1. Mark the quilting lines using the quilting design suggested or your own favorite quilting design. In an effort to imitate the quilting style of the 1930s, we used ¼" parallel lines for the bulk of the quilting on this quilt and a simple cable on the yellow border. Heavy quilting in the muslin areas of each block made the star flowers jump out.

2. Layer the quilt top with batting and backing; baste.

3. Hand quilt following the marked lines.

4. Use the green 2¼"-wide bias strips for binding.

Quilt assembly

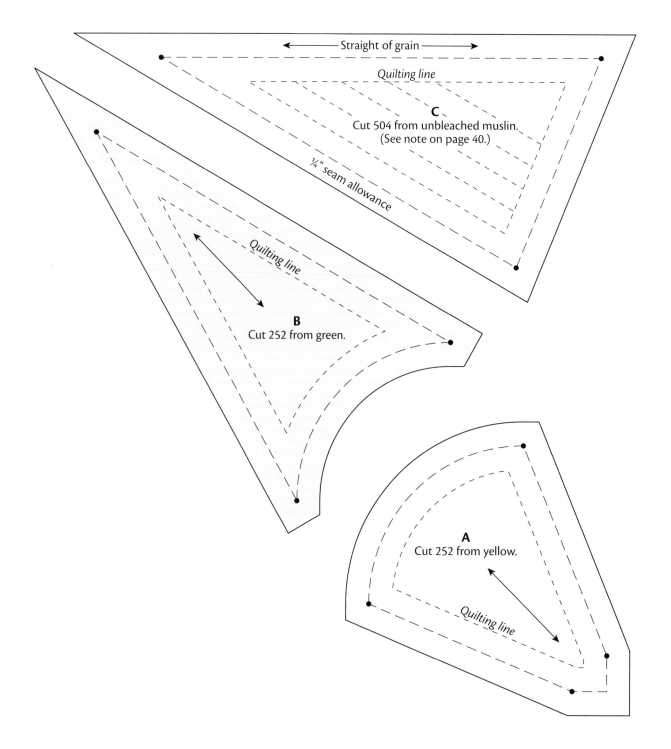

Straight of grain

Quilting line

C
Cut 504 from unbleached muslin.
(See note on page 40.)

¼" seam allowance

Quilting line

B
Cut 252 from green.

A
Cut 252 from yellow.

Quilting line

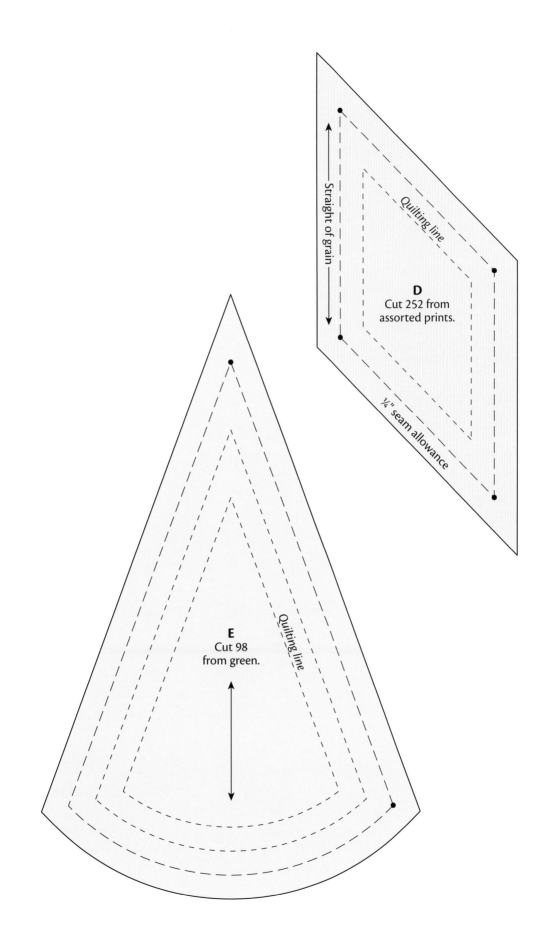

D
Cut 252 from
assorted prints.

Straight of grain

Quilting line

¼" seam allowance

E
Cut 98
from green.

Quilting line

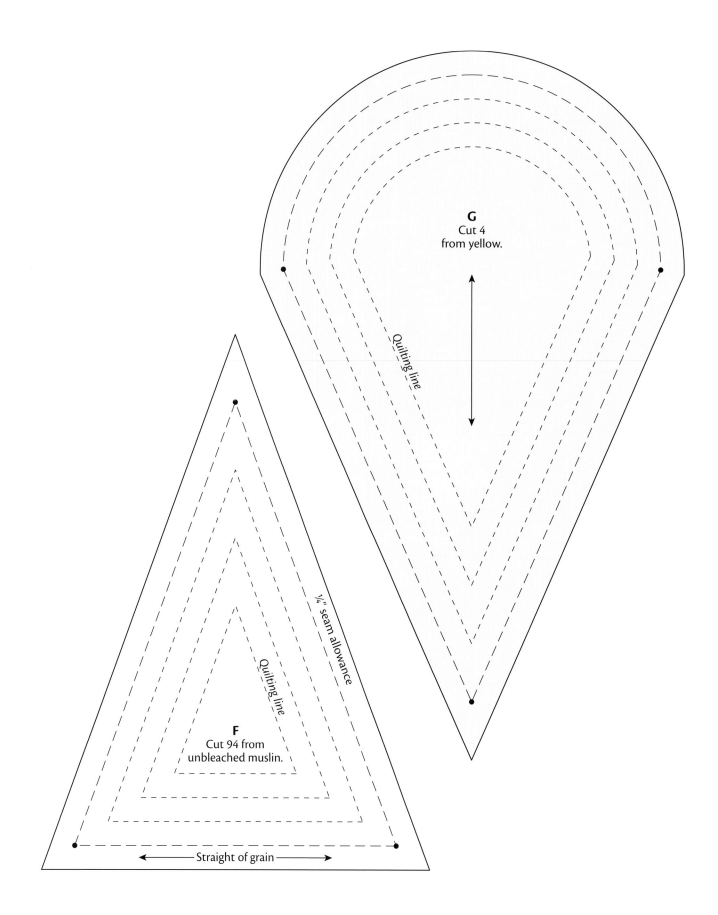

G
Cut 4
from yellow.

Quilting line

¼" seam allowance

Quilting line

F
Cut 94 from
unbleached muslin.

Straight of grain

STAR FLOWER

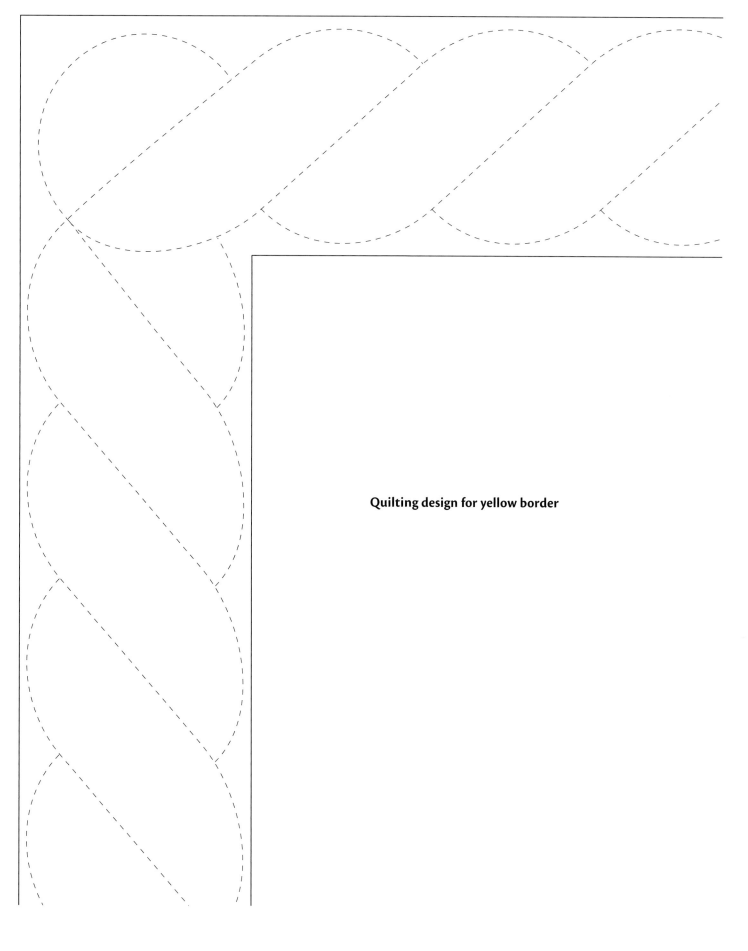

Quilting design for yellow border

As with all the "interlocking" block patterns, this one is deceptively easy. Nancy Page offered this block in a newspaper advertisement in the 1930s for "three cents and a self-addressed, stamped envelope." Ah, for the good old days. We did not have the quilt pattern, but chose to keep it simple. Rotary cutting 2"-wide strips makes this a quick project in both cutting and assembly. With the addition of prairie points and pretty hand quilting, you are done!

Chain Link

Finished Quilt: 72" x 82½" (including prairie points)
Block Size: 10½" x 10½"

MATERIALS

Yardage is based on 42"-wide fabric.

4¾ yards *total* of assorted 1930s reproduction prints for blocks, middle border, and prairie points

3½ yards of unbleached muslin for blocks and borders

2½ yards of 90"-wide muslin for backing*

78" x 89" batting

If using 42"-wide unbleached muslin, you'll need 5½ yards (2 widths pieced vertically).

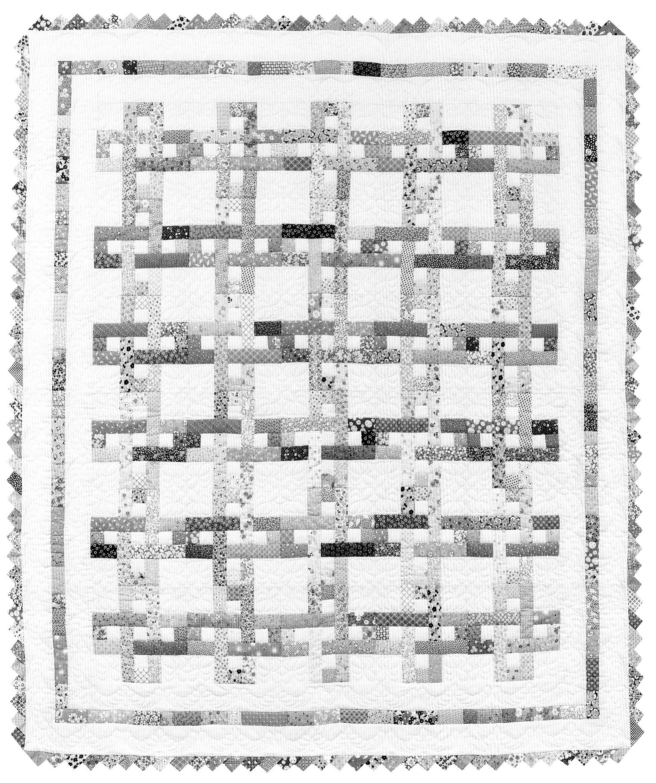

Pieced by Kay Connors and quilted by Karen Earlywine.

CUTTING

All measurements include a ¼"-wide seam allowance.

From the assorted 1930s reproduction prints, cut a *total* of:

44 strips, 2" x 42"; crosscut 37 of *the strips* into:

* 120 rectangles, 2" x 6½"
* 120 rectangles, 2" x 3½"
* 120 squares, 2" x 2"

146 squares, 4" x 4"

From the unbleached muslin, cut:

8 border strips 3¾" x 42"

8 border strips, 3½" x 42"

11 strips, 3½" x 42"; crosscut 120 squares, 3½" x 3½"

8 strips, 2" x 42"; crosscut 150 squares, 2" x 2"

MAKING THE BLOCKS

Each block consists of four rectangular units sewn to a center square using a partial-seam technique.

1. Sew a muslin 2" square to each print 2" square. Press the seam allowance toward the print square. Make 120.

Make 120.

2. Sew a print 2" x 3½" rectangle to the left side of each unit from step 1. Press the seam allowance toward the print rectangle. Make 120.

Make 120.

3. Stitch a muslin 3½" square to the left side of the print rectangle, as shown. Press the seam allowance toward the rectangle. Make 120.

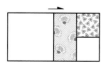

Make 120.

4. Stitch a print 2" x 6½" rectangle to the bottom of the unit from step 3. Press the seam allowance toward the print rectangle. Make 120 rectangle units.

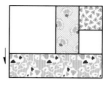

Make 120.

5. Arrange four rectangle units and one muslin 2" square as shown. Sew one rectangle unit to the center square, stopping in the center of the square. Press all seam allowances away from the center square.

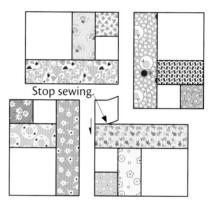

Stop sewing.

6. Sew a rectangle unit to the unit from step 5 as shown; press.

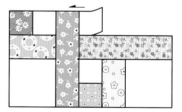

7. Sew the third rectangle unit to the unit from step 6; press.

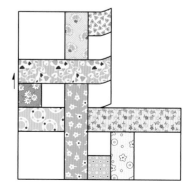

8. Sew the final rectangle unit to the block; press. Sew the small open section of the center-square seam closed to complete the block; press. Make a total of 30 blocks.

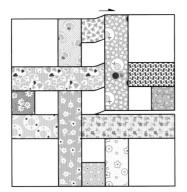

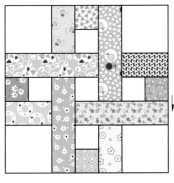

Make 30.

ASSEMBLING THE QUILT TOP

1. Arrange the blocks in six rows of five blocks each as shown in the quilt assembly diagram. Rearrange the blocks until you are pleased with the color placement.

2. Sew the blocks into rows. Press the seam allowances in alternate directions from row to row. Stitch the rows together. Press the seam allowances in one direction.

3. Sew two muslin 3½"-wide strips together end to end to make a long strip. Make four long strips. Refer to "Borders" on page 19. Measure, cut, and sew the muslin border strips to the quilt top for the inner border. Press all seam allowances toward the newly added borders.

4. Using the remaining print 2"-wide strips, cut pieces 2" to 5" long. Randomly sew the pieces together end to end to create two middle-border strips at least 75" long and two middle-border strips at least 60" long.

5. Measure, cut, and sew the shorter strips from step 4 to the top and bottom of the quilt top and the longer strips to the sides of the quilt top for the middle border. Refer to "Borders" as needed. Press all seam allowances toward the newly added borders.

6. Repeat step 3 to sew the muslin 3¾"-wide outer-border strips to the quilt top.

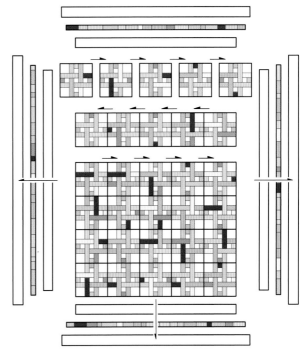

Quilt assembly

QUILTING AND FINISHING

Refer to "Finishing" on page 20 for details as needed.

1. Mark the quilting lines using the quilting design suggested below or your own favorite quilting design.

2. Layer the quilt top with batting and backing; baste.

3. Hand quilt following the marked lines. *Make sure no quilting stitches lie within ½" of the quilt edges to allow for the placement of the prairie points.*

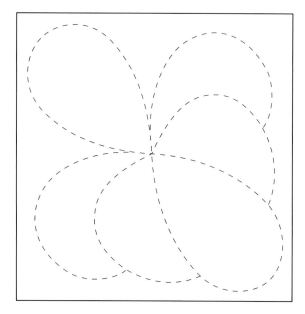

Block corner quilting design

Quilting diagram

ADDING THE PRAIRIE POINTS

When your quilt has been quilted, you will add the prairie points.

1. Trim the batting and backing so that they extend about ⅜" beyond the quilt top on all sides.

2. To make the prairie points, fold each 4" print square in half diagonally, wrong sides together. Fold the square diagonally again, forming a smaller triangle. Make 146 prairie points.

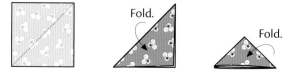

Make 146.

3. Overlap each prairie point by tucking the fold of one point into the opening of the next one. We like a deep overlap, so we overlap the points about half of the length of the first one. This creates a heavy, strong border that lies smooth. You can use fewer prairie points, if you prefer, by not overlapping them as much; just be sure to have the same number of points on each side and the same number of points on the top as on the bottom of the quilt top.

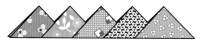

4. Start by placing one point in the center of one side of your quilt, aligning the long cut edge of the triangle with the cut edge of the quilt front. Place a prairie point at each end of the quilt side, making sure that the folded edges of the triangles aim in the same direction as the first one. Arrange prairie points between the triangles until the side of the quilt is full.

We used 34 points each on the top and the bottom and 39 points on each side of the quilt. Pin the prairie points along the edge of the quilt top only.

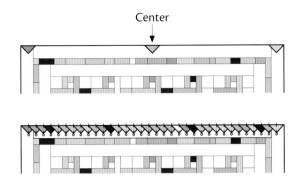

5. On the corners of the quilt, place two points as shown, so that they fit together side by side. They should not overlap. Pin the backing out of the way. Sewing through the quilt top and batting only, stitch the prairie point to all four edges of the quilt using a ¼"-wide seam allowance.

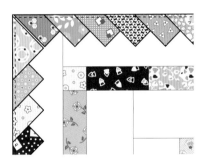

6. Trim the batting close to the stitching. Fold the prairie points out, turning the seam allowance toward the batting, and lightly press on the right side.

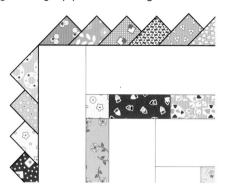

7. Turn the seam allowance of the backing under, covering the seam allowance and the line of stitches on the prairie points, and pin in place. Trim excess fabric at the corners as needed. Finish the back of the quilt using a blind stitch. Add quilting stitches along the edges of the quilt if necessary.

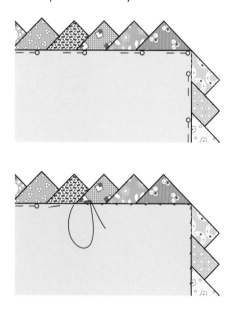

Inner-border quilting design

Outer-border quilting design

The Nancy Page Quilt Club was a regular feature in regional newspapers in the 1930s and it showcased patterns sent in by members. Only the block was shown, but for three cents the full quilt pattern could be ordered. It was suggested that this sweet block could be made in green and yellow, but we thought it was the perfect project for using up those little remnants of prints for the buds coupled with pretty green leaves. We alternated the pieced blocks with plain ones to showcase fine hand quilting, and we created an undulating border of Dresden Plate segments that meander around the blocks.

Finished Quilt: 63½" x 81½" • Block Size: 9" x 9"

MATERIALS

Yardage is based on 42"-wide fabric.

6¾ yards of unbleached muslin for blocks and outer border

3½ yards *total* of assorted 1930s reproduction prints for blocks and border

2¼ yards of green solid for blocks and inner border

2¼ yards of 90"-wide muslin for backing*

70" x 88" piece of batting

Freezer paper

Template plastic

If using 42"-wide unbleached muslin, you'll need 5⅜ yards (2 widths pieced horizontally).

Pieced, appliquéd, and quilted by Kay Connors.

CUTTING

All measurements include a ¼"-wide seam allowance. Template patterns for pieces A, B, C, D, E, and G appear on page 62. For detailed instructions, refer to "Templates" on page 17.

From the *lengthwise grain* of the unbleached muslin, cut:

2 strips, 8½" x 68"

2 strips, 8½" x 66"

From the remaining unbleached muslin, cut:

17 squares, 9½" x 9½"

300" of 2¼"-wide bias binding

72 pieces with template C

72 pieces with template E

From the assorted 1930s reproduction prints, cut a total of:

208 pieces with template G

72 pieces with template A

72 pieces with template B

From the *lengthwise grain* of the green solid, cut:

2 strips, 1½" x 66"

2 strips, 1½" x 50"

144 pieces with template D

NOTE: If you're using a solid fabric, you don't need to cut reverse pieces; however, if you substitute a fabric that has a right and wrong side, cut 72 pieces with template D and 72 pieces with template D reversed.

MAKING THE BLOCKS

You may choose to hand piece the curved seams of this block, making it a relaxing take-along project! Refer to "Curved Seams" on page 16 as needed.

1. Sew the outside curve of a print A piece to the inside curve of each print B piece. Press the seam allowances toward the A piece. Sew a muslin C piece to each A/B unit as shown. Press the seam allowances toward the B piece. Make 72.

Make 72.

2. With right sides together and matching the dots, sew two green D pieces (one regular and one reversed, if applicable) to the unit from step 1 as shown. Start at the outside edge and stop sewing at the dot with a small backstitch. Make 72.

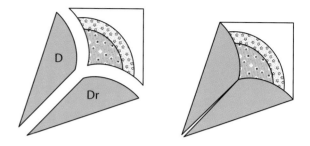

3. Sew the D pieces together, starting at the outside edge and stopping at the dot with a small backstitch. Make sure to keep preceding seam allowances free. Press the center seam allowance to one side and the curved seam allowances toward the D pieces. Make four units for each block (72 total).

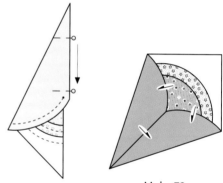

Make 72.

4. Sew a muslin E piece to the right side of each unit from step 3. Press the seam allowances toward the E piece. Make four units for each block (72 total).

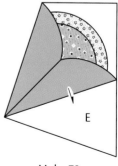

Make 72.

5. Arrange four units as shown. Sew the units together in pairs to make a half-block unit. Sew two half-block units together to complete the block. Press the seam allowances toward the E pieces. Make 18 blocks.

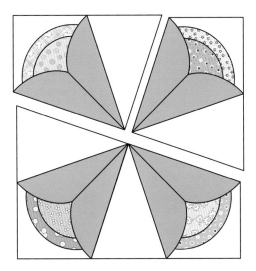

Make 18.

6. Refer to "Basic Appliqué" on page 18. Using template pattern F on page 62, prepare and appliqué a green circle in the center of each block.

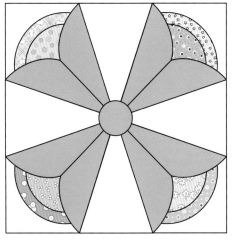

Make 18.

7. On the wrong side of the block, carefully cut a slit in the fabric behind the appliquéd circle. Cut away the excess fabric behind the appliquéd circle, leaving at least a ¼" seam allowance. Remove the freezer-paper template. Make a total of 18 blocks. Trim them to 9½" x 9½", referring to "Squaring Up Blocks" on page 19 as needed.

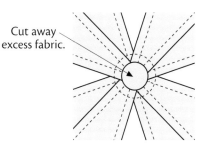

Cut away excess fabric.

lifesaver

Twelve seams come together in the center of this block, creating bulk and making it difficult to make sharp points meet. No problem! That nice member of the Nancy Page Quilt Club provided us with a handy little center disc to appliqué over that potentially ugly spot.

ASSEMBLING THE QUILT TOP

1. Arrange the blocks and muslin 9½" squares into seven rows of five blocks each, alternating the blocks and squares in each row and from row to row as shown in the quilt assembly diagram.

2. Sew the blocks and squares into rows. Press the seam allowances toward the muslin squares. Stitch the rows together. Press the seam allowances in one direction.

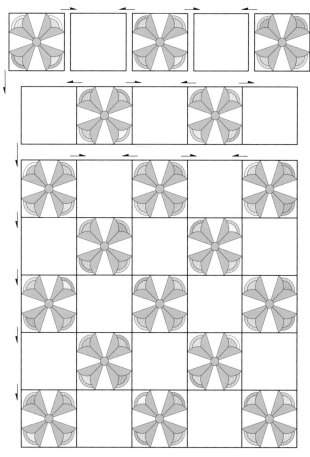

Quilt assembly

3. Refer to "Borders" on page 19. Using the green 1½"-wide strips, measure, cut, and sew the longer strips to the sides of the quilt top and the shorter strips to the top and bottom of the quilt top for the inner border. Press the seam allowances toward the newly added borders.

4. Repeat step 3, sewing the muslin 8½"-wide strips to the quilt top for the outer border. Press the seam allowances toward the green borders.

MAKING THE DRESDEN PLATE BORDER

1. Sew two print G pieces together as shown, starting and stopping at the dots with a small backstitch. Make 104 pairs. Sew two pairs together to make a four-piece unit as shown, starting and stopping at the dots with a small backstitch. Make 52 four-piece units. Press the seam allowances in one direction.

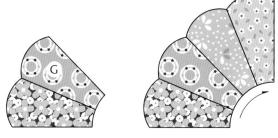

Make 52.

2. Alternating the inside curve as shown, sew the units from step 1 together to make a border strip. Make two border strips with nine units in each strip. Make two border strips with 13 units in each strip. Press the seam allowances in one direction.

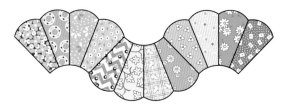

3. Sew two units together to make a half-circle unit for each corner; press. Make a total of four corner units.

Make 4.

4. Refer to the photo on page 57 and the diagram on page 61 as needed. Sew a corner unit to both ends of a long border strip from step 2; press. Sew a short border strip to one of the corner units and stitch a corner unit to the other end of the short border strip. Sew a long border strip to the corner unit, and then stitch the remaining corner unit to the other end of the long strip. At this point you'll have a U shape with

corner units at each open end. Sew one end of the remaining short border strip to each corner unit to complete the rectangular pieced border.

5. Starting in a corner, arrange the pieced border on top of the muslin outer border as shown in the diagram after step 6, adjusting the corners and realigning the sides until you are pleased with the placement. Pin the border in place.

the right pin for the job

During a big appliqué process like this, straight pins will gradually slide out, so small safety pins work best here. As you appliqué, remove a safety pin and replace it with one or more straight pins to stabilize the segment you are working on.

6. Fold under a ³⁄₁₆" seam allowance along both curved edges of the border strip to the wrong side. Appliqué the border in place using the appliqué stitch described on page 18.

7. On the wrong side of the quilt top, carefully cut away the muslin behind the appliquéd border, leaving a ½" seam allowance. Gently press the appliquéd border.

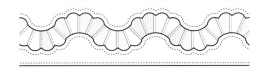

QUILTING AND FINISHING

Refer to "Finishing" on page 20 for details as needed.

1. Mark the quilting lines using the quilting design suggested or your own favorite quilting design. We used a similar quilting design in both the pieced blocks and the plain muslin squares. Look at the finished quilt, and you will see how the lines connect across the blocks. The border is quilted by echoing the undulating border, quilting ⅛" outside the appliquéd edges, and stitching in the ditch along the seam lines of those pieces. We marked the remainder of the border with crosshatch or grid lines, at a 45° angle to the border seams using a ¾" grid, but you can choose a larger one and get a similar effect.

2. Layer the quilt top with batting and backing; baste.

3. Hand quilt following the marked lines.

4. To make the quilt as shown with rounded corners, trim the corners using a dinner plate as a guide. Square up the long edges of the quilt as needed. Machine stitch a scant ¼" from the edge of the quilt. Use the muslin 2¼"-wide bias strips for binding.

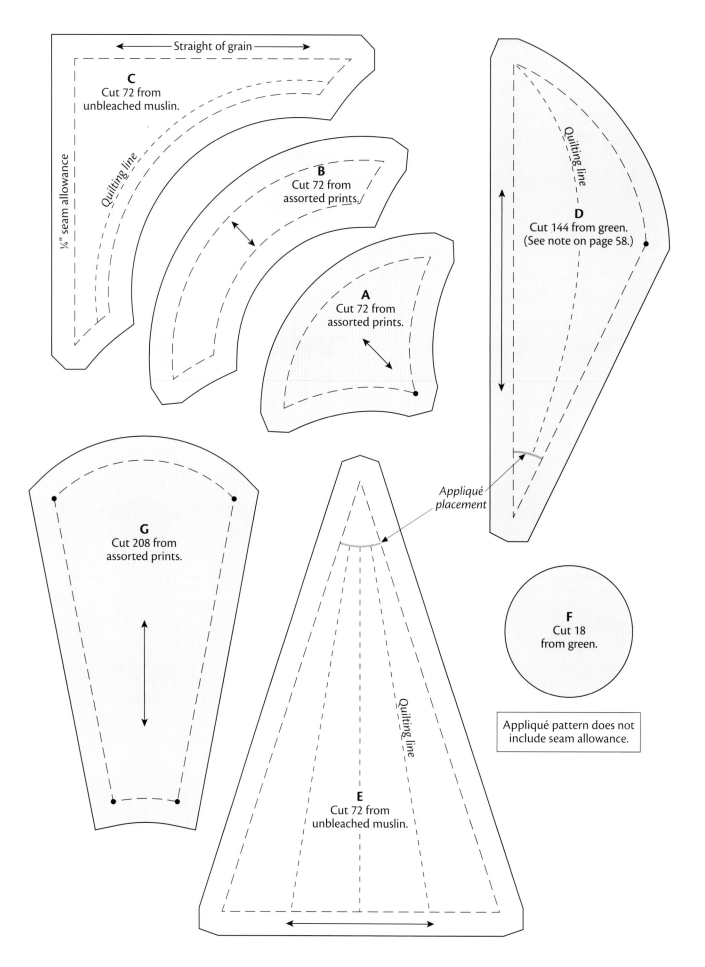

← Straight of grain →

C
Cut 72 from
unbleached muslin.

¼" seam allowance

Quilting line

B
Cut 72 from
assorted prints.

A
Cut 72 from
assorted prints.

D
Cut 144 from green.
(See note on page 58.)

Quilting line

Appliqué placement

G
Cut 208 from
assorted prints.

E
Cut 72 from
unbleached muslin.

Quilting line

Appliqué placement

F
Cut 18
from green.

Appliqué pattern does not
include seam allowance.

Quilting diagram

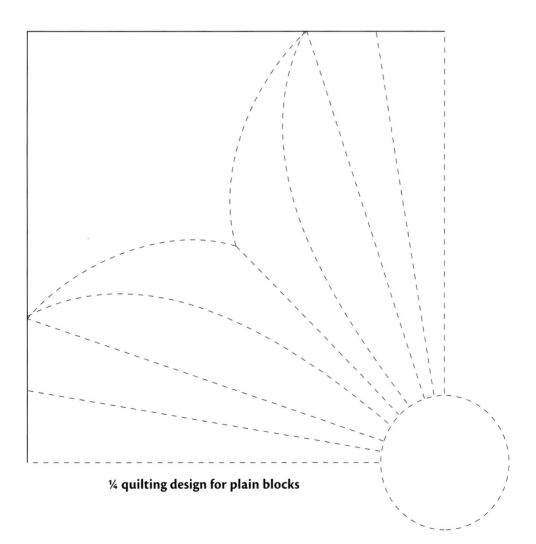

¼ quilting design for plain blocks

An old quilt found faded and in tatters made us want to see it in its original glory. It featured names embroidered on each block, and the rings likely were drafted from dinner plates. We made it in sixteen of our favorite strong solids, letting the rings float above the rest of the quilt and interlock the blocks for a dramatic effect. Extending the quilting around the rings into the outer border created scallops for the border's edge.

Rings 'n' Things

Finished Quilt: 60½" x 60½" • Block Size: 12" x 12"

MATERIALS

Yardage is based on 42"-wide fabric. A fat quarter measures 18" x 21".

4¾ yards of unbleached muslin for blocks, border, and binding

1 fat quarter *each* of 16 solid colors for blocks

2 yards of 90"-wide unbleached muslin for backing*

66" x 66" piece of batting

Template plastic

If using 42"-wide unbleached muslin, you'll need 4 yards (2 widths pieced horizontally).

Pieced and quilted by Kay Connors.

CUTTING

All measurements include a ¼"-wide seam allowance. Template patterns for pieces A, B, and C appear on pages 69 and 70. For detailed instructions, refer to "Templates" on page 17.

From the *lengthwise grain* of the unbleached muslin, cut:

2 strips, 6½" x 63"

2 strips, 6½" x 51"

16 squares, 5½" x 5½"

From the remaining unbleached muslin, cut:

375" of 2¼"-wide bias binding

64 pieces with template B

From *each* of the 16 solid colors, cut:

4 pieces with template A (64 total)

4 pieces with template C (64 total)

MAKING THE BLOCKS

Each block is made using the pieces from one solid color.

1. Sew two A pieces to opposite sides of each muslin square as shown. Press the seam allowances toward the A piece. The A pieces should extend beyond the edges of the square. Sew A pieces to the two remaining sides of the square; press. The center square will float in the middle of the unit. Make 16 units.

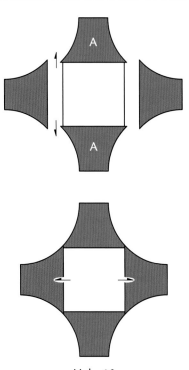

Make 16.

2. Refer to "Curved Seams" on page 16. Sew one muslin B piece to each corner of a unit from step 1, pinning and easing to fit. (The B pieces do not touch the center square.) Press the seam allowances toward the center square.

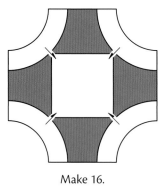

Make 16.

3. Sew C pieces to each corner of the unit as shown, pinning and easing to fit. Press the seam allowances toward the C pieces. Make a total of 16 blocks. Trim them to 12½" x 12½", referring to "Squaring Up Blocks" on page 19 as needed.

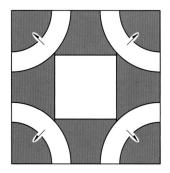

Make 16.

design option

Wouldn't this make a great memory quilt with a photo or message in the center of each block? Make it for any special occasion!

ASSEMBLING THE QUILT TOP

1. Arrange the blocks in four rows of four blocks each as shown in the quilt assembly diagram. Rearrange the blocks until you are pleased with the color placement.

2. Sew the blocks into rows. Press the seam allowances in alternate directions from row to row. Stitch the rows together. Press the seam allowances in one direction.

3. Refer to "Borders" on page 19. Using the muslin 6½"-wide strips, measure, cut, and sew the shorter strips to the top and bottom of the quilt top and the longer strips to the sides of the quilt top for the outer border. Press all seam allowances toward the newly added borders.

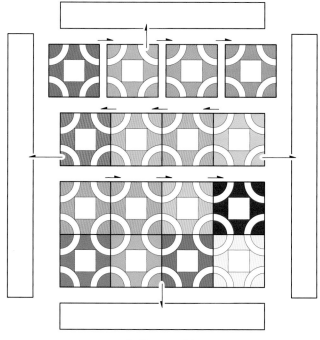

Quilt assembly

4. Use the scallop template pattern on page 71 and template plastic to make a scallop template. Using a removable marker or chalk, trace the scallop edge along the outer border of the quilt. Trace the first scallop, positioning the dot on the template on a block seam as shown in the diagram following step 5.

Move the template to the second position, so that the dot is over the midpoint of an adjacent A piece, and trace the scallop. Continue in this manner marking all four sides of the quilt top.

5. In each corner, position the dot on the scallop template on the outside corner of the block as shown. Trace the scallop, pivoting the template to complete the partial circle.

Do not trim the scallops yet. They will be cut after the quilting is finished.

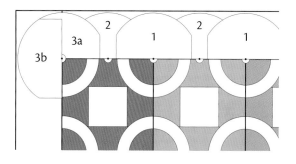

QUILTING AND FINISHING

Refer to "Finishing" on page 20 for details as needed.

1. Mark the quilting lines using the quilting design suggested on page 68 or your own favorite quilting design.

2. Layer the quilt top with batting and backing; baste.

3. Hand quilt following the marked lines.

4. Machine stitch a scant ¼" from the marked line. Cut the scallops along the marked lines. Use the muslin 2¼"-wide bias strips for binding.

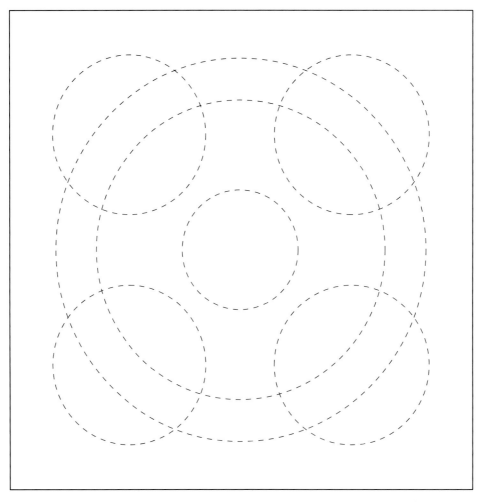

Quilting design for block center

Quilting diagram

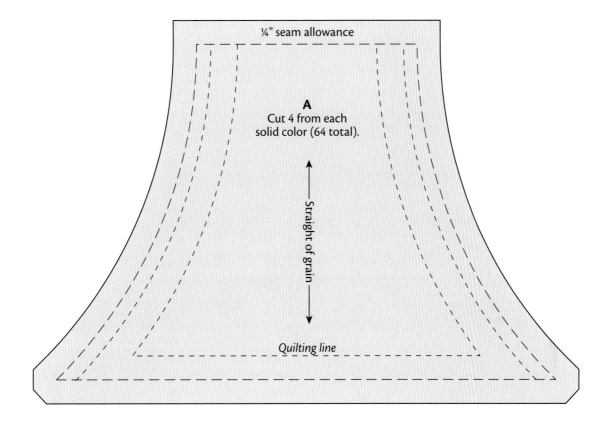

¼" seam allowance

A
Cut 4 from each
solid color (64 total).

Straight of grain

Quilting line

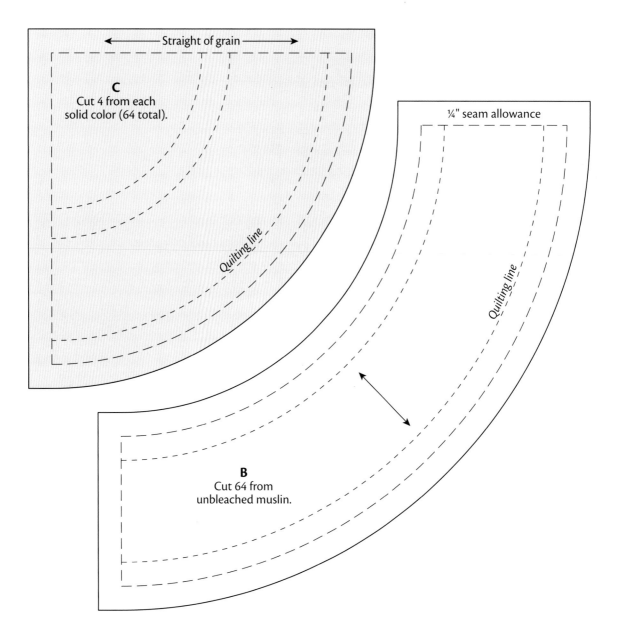

Straight of grain

C
Cut 4 from each
solid color (64 total).

Quilting line

¼" seam allowance

Quilting line

B
Cut 64 from
unbleached muslin.

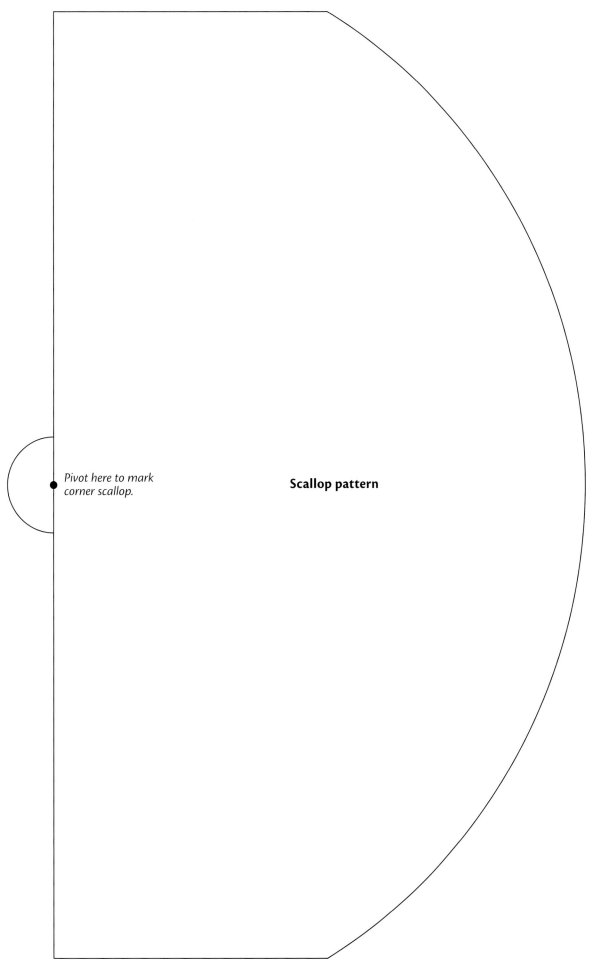

Pivot here to mark corner scallop.

Scallop pattern

"Box Quilt" was the original name of this block from the Nancy Page Quilt Club, clipped during the 1930s from the *Spokane Daily Chronicle* newspaper. We rearranged the prints and solids to feature an all-print star in the middle of the block and used strong solid colors in the corners to frame each star to achieve the "Attic Windows" effect. Plain sashing and bold border strips with diagonal lines of quilting finish this bright quilt. The window effect necessitated the preservation of the diagonal corner seams, so some skill with set-in pieces is a must.

Stars in the Attic

Finished Quilt: 79½" x 93½" • Block Size: 12" x 12"

MATERIALS

Yardage is based on 42"-wide fabric.

2½ yards of unbleached muslin for the blocks and sashing

2 yards *total* of assorted 1930s reproduction prints for blocks (choose colors that coordinate with the solid colors)

1¾ yards *total* of assorted solids for blocks

1 yard of lavender print for outer border

¾ yard of green print for fourth border

¾ yard of yellow print for third border

¾ yard of red print for second border

⅝ yard of blue print for first border

¾ yard of orange print for binding

3⅛ yards of 90"-wide muslin for backing*

86" x 100" piece of batting

Template plastic

*If using 42"-wide unbleached muslin, you'll need 8 yards (3 widths pieced horizontally).

Pieced and quilted by Kay Connors.

CUTTING

All measurements include a ¼"-wide seam allowance. Template patterns for pieces A and B appear on page 79. For detailed instructions, refer to "Templates" on page 17.

From the *lengthwise grain* of the unbleached muslin, cut:

2 strips, 2½" x 71"

2 strips, 2½" x 61"

4 strips, 2½" by 57"

15 strips, 2½" x 12½"

40 squares, 3¾" x 3¾"; cut once diagonally to yield 80 half-square triangles

80 squares, 2½" x 2½"

From the assorted solids, cut a total of:

160 pieces with A (Cut in pairs, one regular and one reversed, if applicable.)*

From the assorted 1930s reproduction print fabrics, cut a total of:

80 pieces with template A

80 pieces with template B

From the blue print, cut:

7 strips, 2½" x 42"

From the red print, cut:

8 strips, 2½" x 42"

From the yellow print, cut:

8 strips, 2½" x 42"

From the green print, cut:

8 strips, 2½" x 42"

From the lavender print, cut:

9 strips, 3" x 42"

From the orange print, cut:

9 strips, 2¼" x 42"

*NOTE: If you're using muslin or a solid fabric, you don't need to cut reverse pieces; however, if you substitute a fabric that has a right and wrong side, cut 80 pieces with template A and 80 pieces with template A reversed.

MAKING THE BLOCKS

1. On the wrong side of the muslin squares and triangles, place a dot in one corner of each square and the right-angle corner of each triangle ¼" from the raw edge in preparation for Y-seam construction.

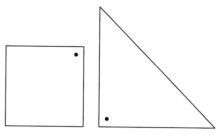

Mark corners ¼" from edge.

2. Refer to "Set-In Pieces and Y Seams" on page 15. Arrange two solid A pieces (one regular and one reversed, if applicable) and a muslin square as shown. Place the two A pieces right sides together and sew the seam, starting at the outside edge and stopping at the dot with a small backstitch. Press the seam allowance to one side.

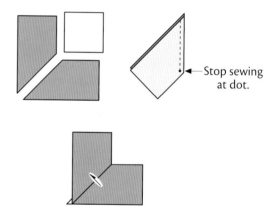

←Stop sewing at dot.

3. Sew the muslin square to the A unit from step 2, starting with a small backstitch at the dot and sewing to the outside edges. Press the seam allowances toward the A units.

4. Sew a print A piece to the unit from step 3 as shown. Press the seam allowances toward the print A piece.

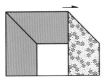

5. Sew a print B piece to the unit from step 4 as shown. Press the seam allowances toward the B piece. Make a total of 80 units.

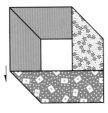

Make 80.

6. Arrange four units as shown. Sew the units together in pairs, starting at the outside edge and stopping at the dot with a small backstitch. Press the seam allowances toward the B pieces. Sew the pairs together, starting and stopping at the dot with a small backstitch; press. Make 20.

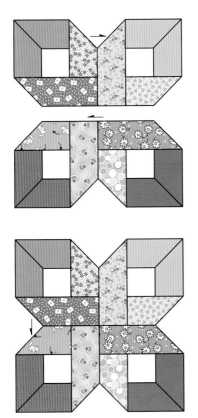

Make 20.

7. Arrange a unit from step 6 and four marked triangles as shown. Sew a triangle to each side of the unit, referring to "Set-In Pieces and Y Seams" as needed. Press the seam allowances away from the triangles. Make a total of 20 blocks. Trim them to 12½" x 12½", referring to "Squaring Up Blocks" on page 19, as needed.

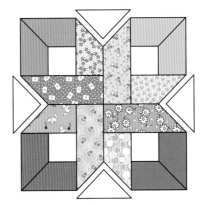

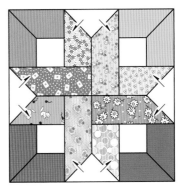

Make 20.

ASSEMBLING THE QUILT TOP

1. Arrange the blocks in five rows of four blocks each as shown in the quilt assembly diagram. Rearrange the blocks until you are pleased with the color placement.

digital help

Anytime you have pieces or blocks laid out in a pleasing arrangement and have to pick them up or take them off your design wall before the project is completed, just take a picture with your digital camera. When you are ready to resume, you don't even have to print the picture—just find the shot and look at the view window of your camera for reference.

2. To make each horizontal block row, sew together four blocks and three muslin 2½" x 12½" sashing strips, alternating them as shown. Press the seam allowances toward the muslin. Make five block rows.

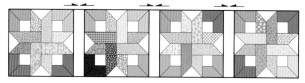

Make 5.

3. Measure the length of each of the five block rows. If they differ, calculate the average and consider this the length. Trim the muslin 57"-long strips to the length of your row measurement. Make four sashing strips.

4. Sew the block rows and the four sashing strips from step 3 together, alternating them as shown. Press the seam allowances toward the sashing strips.

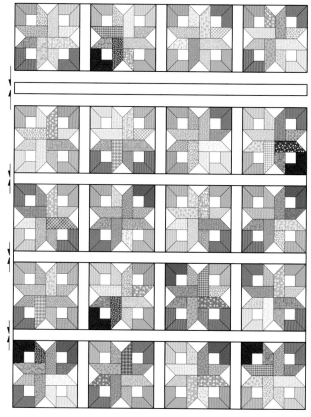

Quilt assembly

5. Refer to "Borders" on page 19. Using the remaining muslin 2½"-wide strips, measure, cut, and sew the longer strips to the sides of the quilt top and the shorter strips to the top and bottom of the quilt top. Press all seam allowances toward the muslin strips.

6. Sew the blue 2½"-wide strips together end to end to make a continuous strip. Measure, cut, and sew the strips to the sides of the quilt top and then to the top and bottom of the quilt top for the first border. Press all seam allowances toward the newly added strips.

7. Repeat step 6 to sew border strips to the quilt top in the following order:
   - Red strips for the second border
   - Yellow strips for the third border
   - Green strips for the fourth border
   - Lavender strips for the outer border

QUILTING AND FINISHING

Refer to "Finishing" on page 20 for details as needed.

1. Mark the quilting lines using the quilting design suggested on page 78 or your own favorite quilting design. For the print borders, using our longest ruler, we placed the 45° line on the ruler along the seam line next to the muslin border. Using a removable marker we made two parallel lines, ¼" apart, and placed the set of lines 1" apart.

2. Layer the quilt top with batting and backing; baste.

3. Hand quilt following the marked lines.

4. Use the orange 2¼"-wide strips for binding.

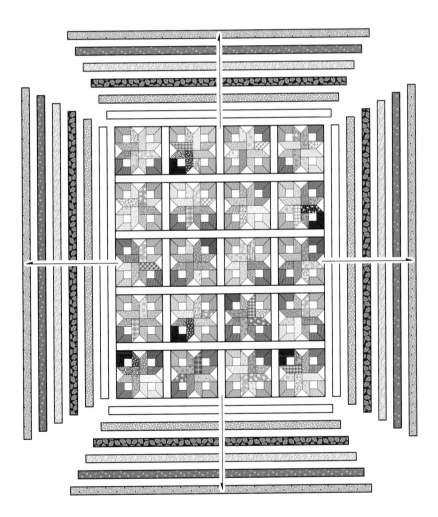

Quilting diagram

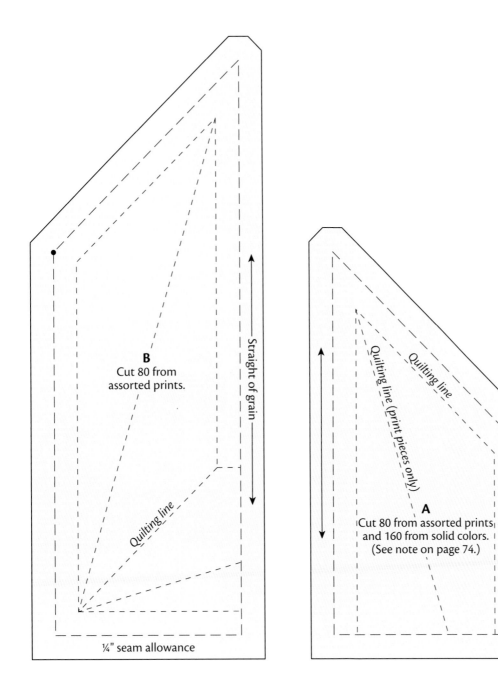

B
Cut 80 from
assorted prints.

Straight of grain

Quilting line

¼" seam allowance

Quilting line

Quilting line (print pieces only)

A
Cut 80 from assorted prints
and 160 from solid colors.
(See note on page 74.)

We would love to tell you this is an easy pattern! After all, there are no curved seams, no appliqués, no set-in pieces—but there are lots of points to match, so careful cutting and sewing are a must! Achieve perfection, and we bow to your superior piecing talents. However, if perfection eludes you, then approach this as a "gallop and grin" project. (If you can gallop by on a horse and don't see any imperfections, you can grin about it.) We added solid-color corners to the hexagon-shaped quilt to form a rectangle and provide a perfect canvas to show off your hand quilting.

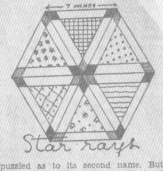

Sweet Insanity

Finished Quilt: 67½" x 79" • Block Size: 7"
(each side of the equilateral triangle)

MATERIALS

Yardage is based on 42"-wide fabric. A fat eighth measures 9" x 21".

3 yards of unbleached muslin for the blocks and inner border

2⅜ yards *total* or 150 squares, 5½" x 5½", of assorted 1930s reproduction prints for blocks

2⅜ yards of red solid for setting corners, outer border, and binding

¾ yard *total* or 1 fat eighth *each* of 8 to 10 assorted solids for blocks

2½ yards of 90"-wide unbleached muslin for backing*

74" x 85" batting

Template plastic

*If using 42"-wide unbleached muslin, you'll need 5¼ yards
(2 widths pieced vertically).*

Pieced and quilted by Kay Connors.

CUTTING

All measurements include a ¼"-wide seam allowance. Template patterns for pieces A, B, and C appear on page 85. For detailed instructions, refer to "Templates" on page 17.

From the assorted 1930s reproduction prints, cut a *total* of:

150 pieces with template A

From the unbleached muslin, cut:

6 strips, 1½" x 42"

65 strips, 1¼" x 42"; cut into 450 pieces with template B

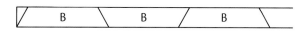

From the fat eighths of 8 to 10 assorted solids, cut a *total* of:

450 pieces with template C

From the red solid, cut:

8 strips, 3" x 42"

8 strips, 2¼" x 42"

2 rectangles, 19" x 33"; cut each rectangle once diagonally to yield 4 wedge pieces

MAKING THE BLOCKS

1. Sew one muslin B piece to a print A piece as shown to make a no-diamond unit. Press the seam allowances toward the B piece. Make 150 units.

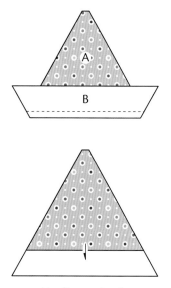

No-diamond unit.
Make 150.

2. Sew one solid C piece to a muslin B piece as shown to make a one-diamond unit. Press the seam allowances toward the B piece. Make 150 units.

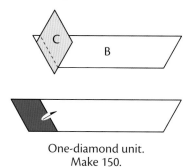

One-diamond unit.
Make 150.

3. Sew a solid C piece to each end of a muslin B piece to make a two-diamond unit. Press the seam allowances toward the B piece. Make 150 units.

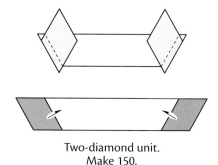

Two-diamond unit.
Make 150.

4. Sew a one-diamond unit to each no-diamond unit, carefully matching the seams. Press the seam allowances away from the print triangle and trim the dog-ears. Make 150.

Make 150.

SWEET INSANITY

5. Sew a two-diamond unit to each unit from step 4, carefully matching the seams. Press the seam allowances away from the print and trim. Make a total of 150 triangle blocks.

Make 150.

ASSEMBLING THE QUILT TOP

Do not try to set the triangle blocks together as shown by Nancy Page on page 80. This would create a nightmare of set-in pieces.

1. Referring to the assembly diagram, arrange the triangle blocks in rows. Rows 1 and 10 use 11 triangle blocks each; then add two blocks for each subse-

quent row so that center rows 5 and 6 each use 19 triangle blocks.

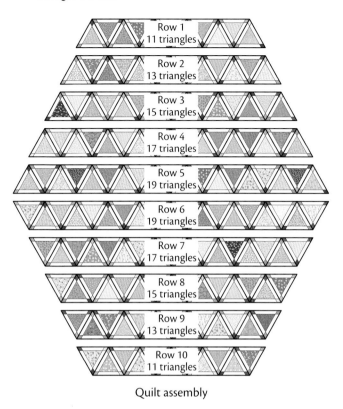

Quilt assembly

2. Sew the blocks together in rows, carefully matching the seams. Make sure there is a ¼" seam allowance where three diamonds meet to form a half star. Press the seam allowances in one direction.

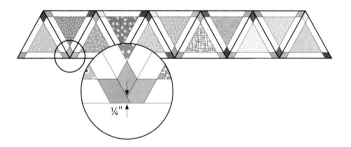

3. Sew the rows together, carefully matching the seams, to make a large hexagon. Press the seam allowances open and trim the dog-ears.

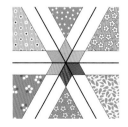

4. Center a muslin 1½"-wide strip along each side of the hexagon, right sides together, and stitch in place. Press the seam allowances toward the muslin strips. When all six strips are sewn, trim the muslin strips to fit the hexagon shape.

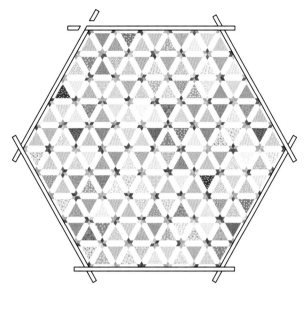

a fun tablecloth

You could stop at this point and have a great hexagonal tablecloth. Simply bind or hem the large hexagon that you have created and you are done.

5. Maintaining a 30° angle, sew the red wedges to the top and bottom of the hexagon as shown to make a rectangular quilt top. The wedges will overlap in the middle. Trim any excess fabric and press the seam allowances toward the red wedges. Use a large square ruler to square up each corner and a long ruler to trim a straight line across the top and bottom edges of the quilt top as needed.

6. Refer to "Borders" on page 19. Measure, cut, and sew the red 3"-wide strips to the sides of the quilt top and then the top and bottom of the quilt top for the outer border. Press all seam allowances toward the newly added strips.

QUILTING AND FINISHING

Refer to "Finishing" on page 20 for details as needed.

1. Mark the quilting lines using the quilting design suggested below or your own favorite quilting design. Use the 30° and 60° marks on a long ruler and a removable marker to extend the lines formed by the triangle seams to the outside edges of the quilt. Use the small triangle template to mark an inverted triangle in each print triangle.

2. Layer the quilt top with batting and backing; baste.

3. Hand quilt following the marked lines.

4. Use the red 2¼"-wide strips for binding.

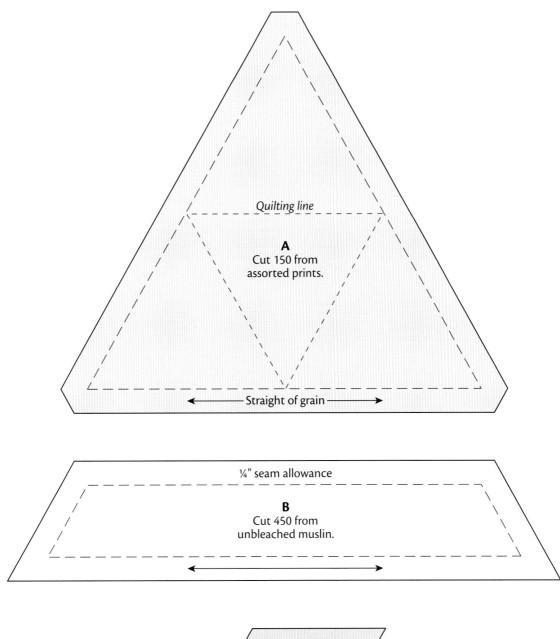

Quilting line

A
Cut 150 from
assorted prints.

←——— Straight of grain ———→

¼" seam allowance

B
Cut 450 from
unbleached muslin.

←————————→

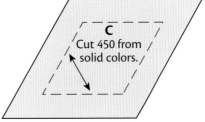

C
Cut 450 from
solid colors.

Quilting diagram

SWEET INSANITY

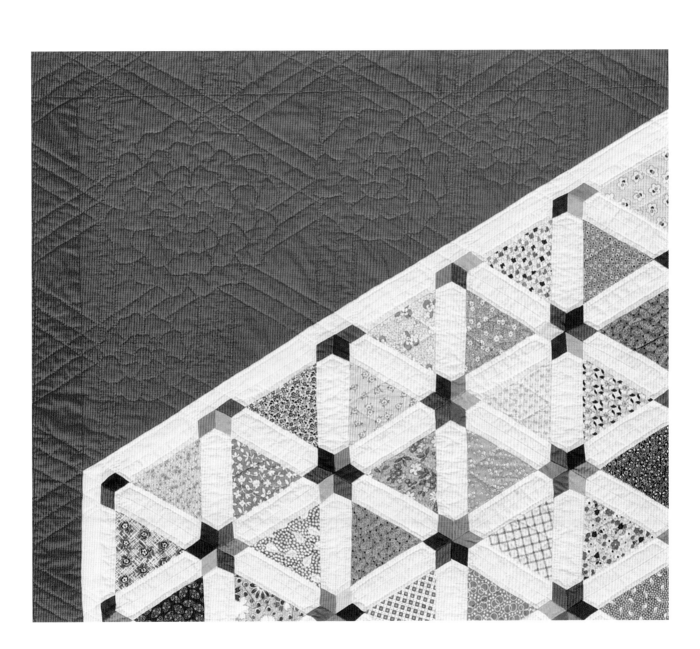

With names and the year 1931 embroidered on it, this old quilt was the obvious choice for a quilt commemorating our family get-together. We pieced the individual blocks, took them along for signing, got family members to do the embroidery, and set the blocks together without borders or sashing. Simple outline quilting and stars, celebrating our Texas heritage, give our quilt the dimension it needs.

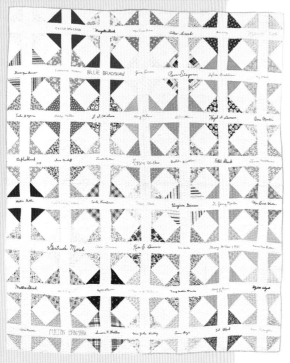

Reunion Memories

Finished Quilt: 58" x 69½" • Finished Block: 11½" x 11½"

MATERIALS

Yardage is based on 42" wide fabric. A fat eighth measures 9" x 21".

1 fat eighth *each* of 30 assorted 1930s reproduction prints for blocks

3½ yards of unbleached muslin for block backgrounds

⅝ yard of fabric for binding

2 yards of 90"-wide unbleached muslin for backing*

64" x 76" piece of batting

Freezer paper

If using 42"-wide unbleached muslin, you'll need 4 yards (2 widths pieced horizontally).

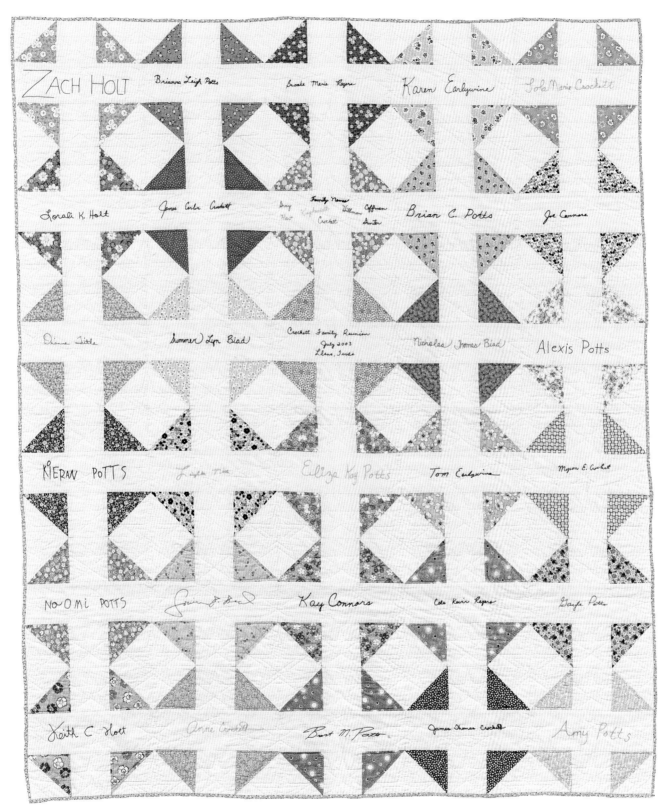

Pieced and quilted by Kay Connors and Karen Earlywine.

CUTTING

All measurements include a ¼"-wide seam allowance.

From *each* of the 30 assorted 1930s reproduction prints, cut:

2 squares, 4⅞" x 4⅞"; cut once diagonally to yield 4 half-square triangles (120 total)

From the unbleached muslin, cut:

3 strips, 12" x 42"; crosscut into 30 rectangles, 4" x 12"

8 strips, 4⅞" x 42"; crosscut into 60 squares, 4⅞" x 4⅞". Cut each square once diagonally to yield 120 triangles.

6 strips, 4½" x 42"; crosscut into 60 rectangles, 4" x 4½"

From the binding fabric, cut:

7 strips, 2¼" x 42"

From the freezer paper, cut:

30 pieces, 3" x 10"

MAKING THE BLOCKS

1. Sew print triangles and muslin triangles together along their long edges to make half-square-triangle units. Press the seam allowances toward the print triangles. Make four matching units for each block (120 total).

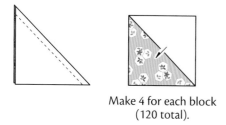

Make 4 for each block (120 total).

2. Sew matching half-square-triangle units to each long side of a muslin 4" x 4½" rectangle as shown. Press the seam allowances toward the muslin rectangle. Make two matching units for each block (60 total).

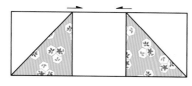

Make 2 for each block (60 total).

3. Sew matching units from step 2 to each long side of a muslin 4" x 12" rectangle to complete the block. Press the seam allowances toward the muslin rectangle. Make a total of 30 blocks. Trim them to 12" x 12", referring to "Squaring Up Blocks" on page 19, as needed.

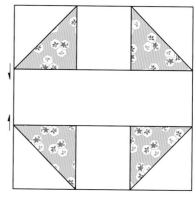

Make 30.

ADDING SIGNATURES

1. On the wrong side of each finished block, center and press a piece of freezer paper (with the shiny side facing down) in the middle of the large muslin rectangle.

2. If you plan to embroider the names, have each person sign the blocks with a pencil. If you want to skip the embroidery, use a permanent maker. Encourage your signers to stay in the middle of the block so that you can maintain the seam allowances around the outside edges of the blocks.

practice signing

Prepare some extra pieces of muslin with freezer paper so that your signers can practice before signing the finished block. This is especially helpful when using a permanent marker. Better to discard a few pieces of muslin than have to remake the blocks.

3. After the blocks are signed, remove the freezer paper. Using a stem stitch and two strands of embroidery floss, embroider the names.

ASSEMBLING THE QUILT TOP

1. Arrange the blocks in six rows of five blocks each as shown in the quilt assembly diagram. Rearrange the blocks until you are pleased with the color placement.

2. Sew the blocks into rows. Press the seam allowances in alternate directions from row to row. Stitch the rows together. Press the seam allowances in one direction.

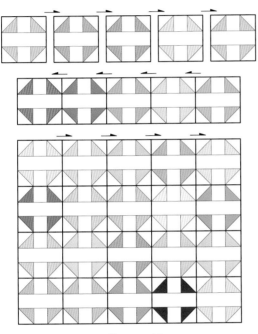

Quilt assembly

QUILTING AND FINISHING

Refer to "Finishing" on page 20 for details as needed.

1. Mark the quilting lines using the star motifs on page 92 or your own favorite quilting design. We quilted ¼" from the seam lines in all the print triangles and randomly quilted stars in all the muslin areas.

2. Layer the quilt top with batting and backing; baste.

3. Hand quilt following the marked lines.

4. Use the 2¼"-wide strips for binding.

quilting suggestion

You will find that many of your signers write very tiny or off to one side, and you can quilt a star or two in the areas they left blank.

Quilting designs

Quilting diagram

About the Authors

KAY
CONNORS

Kay Connors was born in Texas, raised in New Mexico, and she has had homes in Colorado, California, Washington, Alaska (where she co-owned a fabric store), and Idaho, where she has lived since 1979. Hopelessly lost in the 1930s, she has been quilting since 1973, first to use up fabric, and then to feed her passion. She is a contemporary quilter, but finds she can't pass up anything having to do with old quilts. She buys feed sacks, old quilt tops, quilts, and every piece of reproduction '30s fabric she finds. Collecting old patterns and drafting her own from found quilts has allowed her to make quilts that she feels need to be in her home.

Making quilts both for competition and for her large family of four married children and nine grandchildren, she always has a list of projects waiting. Kay is a past officer in both Thimble Collectors International and Nimble Fingers Thimble Club, organizations for collectors of antique sewing tools. She recently retired from office management and realized that she finally had time to do "that quilt book" she and her sister had often talked about writing.

In 1998, Kay and her sister Karen bought a little house in the hill country of Texas as a quilting getaway. They renovated and decorated it with all things '30s from Depression glass and Fiesta ware to mission oak and quilts, quilts, quilts—most collected, but some newly made, or finally-quilted old tops. Only one quilt in the house was inherited.

KAREN
EARLYWINE

Karen Earlywine was the youngest of four children in a post–World War II family in Texas. She was two years old when the family moved to New Mexico. Karen, her husband, and their grown children still live in the southwestern part of the state. She has been teaching both in the public schools and part time at the university level for more than 35 years.

Quilting became an important part of her life in 1977. Her first quilt was "interesting" because there was little information available on the subject, and finding fabrics that were suited for quilts was a serious problem. She tried to solve that problem by opening a fabric/quilt shop with a friend. They had a great time, but finally had to recognize that they were way ahead of the time starting such a shop in a small town.

Now the most important thing in Karen's life is her family. Four young grandchildren have new quilts as they go from cradles to cribs to beds. College graduations and other events in the lives of close friends and family are celebrated with the gift of a quilt.

Years of working on old homes and collecting antiques intensified the interest Karen has in reproduction fabrics and quilts of the past. She and her sister both share this passion and try to get away to their shared house in Texas to scour the area for fabric and antique treasures as often as possible. Fabric exchange is a frequent recreational activity.

New and Bestselling Titles from

America's Best-Loved
Quilt Books®

America's Best-Loved Craft & Hobby Books®
America's Best-Loved Knitting Books®

APPLIQUÉ
Applique Quilt Revival
Beautiful Blooms
Cutting-Garden Quilts
Dream Landscapes—*NEW!*
More Fabulous Flowers
Sunbonnet Sue and Scottie Too

BABIES AND CHILDREN
Baby's First Quilts—*NEW!*
Baby Wraps
Even More Quilts for Baby
Let's Pretend—*NEW!*
The Little Box of Baby Quilts
Snuggle-and-Learn Quilts for Kids
Sweet and Simple Baby Quilts

BEGINNER
Color for the Terrified Quilter
Happy Endings, Revised Edition
Machine Appliqué for the Terrified Quilter
Your First Quilt Book (or it should be!)

GENERAL QUILTMAKING
Adventures in Circles
American Jane's Quilts for All Seasons—*NEW!*
Bits and Pieces
Charmed
Cool Girls Quilt
Country-Fresh Quilts—*NEW!*
Creating Your Perfect Quilting Space
Follow-the-Line Quilting Designs Volume Three
Gathered from the Garden
The New Handmade—*NEW!*
Points of View
Positively Postcards
Prairie Children and Their Quilts
Quilt Revival
A Quilter's Diary
Quilter's Happy Hour
Quilting for Joy—*NEW!*
Sensational Sashiko
Simple Seasons
Skinny Quilts and Table Runners

Twice Quilted
Young at Heart Quilts

HOLIDAY AND SEASONAL
Christmas Quilts from Hopscotch
Christmas with Artful Offerings
Comfort and Joy
Holiday Wrappings

HOOKED RUGS, NEEDLE FELTING, AND PUNCHNEEDLE
The Americana Collection
Miniature Punchneedle Embroidery
Needle-Felting Magic
Needle Felting with Cotton and Wool
Punchneedle Fun

PAPER PIECING
Easy Reversible Vests, Revised Edition—*NEW!*
Paper-Pieced Mini Quilts
Show Me How to Paper Piece
Showstopping Quilts to Foundation Piece
A Year of Paper Piecing

PIECING
501 Rotary-Cut Quilt Blocks—*NEW!*
Better by the Dozen
Favorite Traditional Quilts Made Easy—*NEW!*
Loose Change—*NEW!*
Maple Leaf Quilts
Mosaic Picture Quilts
New Cuts for New Quilts
Nine by Nine
On-Point Quilts
Quiltastic Curves
Ribbon Star Quilts
Rolling Along
Sew One and You're Done

QUICK QUILTS
40 Fabulous Quick-Cut Quilts
Instant Bargello
Quilts on the Double
Sew Fun, Sew Colorful Quilts

SCRAP QUILTS
Nickel Quilts
Save the Scraps
Simple Strategies for Scrap Quilts
Spotlight on Scraps

CRAFTS
Art from the Heart
The Beader's Handbook
Card Design
Crochet for Beaders
Dolly Mama Beads
Embellished Memories—*NEW!*
Friendship Bracelets All Grown Up
Making Beautiful Jewelry—*NEW!*
Paper It!—*NEW!*
Sculpted Threads
Sew Sentimental
Trading Card Treasures—*NEW!*

KNITTING & CROCHET
365 Crochet Stitches a Year
365 Knitting Stitches a Year
A to Z of Knitting
All about Knitting—*NEW!*
Amigurumi World
Beyond Wool—*NEW!*
Cable Confidence
Casual, Elegant Knits
Chic Knits
Crocheted Pursenalities
Gigi Knits…and Purls
Kitty Knits
Knitted Finger Puppets—*NEW!*
The Knitter's Book of Finishing Techniques
Knitting Circles around Socks
Knitting with Gigi
More Sensational Knitted Socks
Pursenalities
Skein for Skein
Toe-Up Techniques for Hand Knit Socks, Revised Edition—*NEW!*
Together or Separate—*NEW!*

Our books are available at bookstores and your favorite craft, fabric, and yarn retailers. If you don't see the title you're looking for, visit us at **www.martingale-pub.com** or contact us at:

1-800-426-3126

International: 1-425-483-3313
Fax: 1-425-486-7596 • Email: info@martingale-pub.com

9/08